THE TREES AND ME

Florence Hardesty

To Ralph and Nancy
Jean,

Enjoy

Florence Hardesty

Feb. 6, 1999

Silver Tree Books   Silverton, Oregon

Silver Tree Books
Box 707
Silverton,Oregon 97381

© 1999 by Florence Hardesty

ISBN 0-9631769-2-7

Library of Congress Catalog Card Number: 98-88709

Cover by Sheila Somerville

Design by DIMI PRESS

Typeface - 12 pt. Palatino

Acknowledgments

I am indebted to all the people who made this book possible. First, there are the people who have become characters in my small true dramas.

The most important is my husband, Verl Holden, who says he has no secrets since writing became one of my vocations. He doesn't object to making his own dinner when I am off selling books and he dutifully carts heavy boxes of books out to my car. He even sells them to anyone who happens by. (Although this may be because he wants those darn boxes out of the closet.) Besides all this, he is my greatest support and most loyal fan.

My daughters and sons-in-law also deserve thanks. Susan and James Irvine, and Shevawn Hardesty and George Arnos are fans as well as characters and I am grateful. My stepson, Paul Holden, who spends most of his day in the nursery office, keeps me from being lonely and occasionally appears in my stories. My mother-in-law, Ruby Holden, provided one of my best stories and serves as an inspiration to me as I look forward to old age.

My late sister-in-law, Patricia Huskey told me about the way her husband, James Huskey, handled the pesky chickens that plagued her mother. Thanks, Dear Sister. I miss you.

My late brother, John Fisher, told me how he spent the 50th anniversary of D-Day and provided me with other stories. Thanks Johnny.

Our good friends and fellow nurserymen, Sally and Dick Bush, told me about a number of incidents that became some of my best stories.

My husband's employees, and my good friends, Isidera Villegas, Javier Lara, Ernesto Santos, and Antonio Garcia, keep the nursery running smoothly and are mentioned occasionally. The other employees aren't mentioned by name but are important to the book and the nursery.

I want to acknowledge the contributions to the people who helped create the book. Cindy Wall took time from her own writing to act as my editor and Robert Wall served as copy editor. Sheila Somerville designed the cover. Dick and Mary Lutz of Dimi Press prepared the book for the press.

Contents

Introduction

This book is a sequel to *Down on the Tree Farm*, which was written several years ago. That book is an account of how a clean handed nursing professor (that's me) met and fell in love with a nurseryman, a man of the soil, and married him. Moving to the farm was an adventure which was saved from being a disaster only by our deep affection for each other and the wicked sense of humor that each of us possesses. Every week or so since that book was published something happened at the wholesale nursery where my husband, Verl Holden, and I live which would drive me to my computer. The something might be a humorous experience, or a not so humorous one that became funny as the weeks passed.It might also be a thought or a strongly held opinion that was stimulated by the morning paper. I've picked the best of these for this book. Many of the chapters have appeared in the *Capital Press* in my column *On the Tree Farm*.

Verl and I have been married for almost twenty years and our relationship is still a source of wonder and happiness. I have retired from the Oregon Health Sciences University, but hold emeritus status and am delighted when I am asked to teach an occasional class. I closed my psychotherapy practice several years ago and have devoted myself to writing.

Verl's son, Paul, has joined his father's business and handles the office work, the phone and much of the selling. His father is happy to be freed of that work, which to him was an annoyance, and be able to work in the fields or at the propagation bench. Kristi, Verl's daughter, is working in Portland. My daughters, Susan and Shevawn, and their husbands live in the East and are busy with their careers and raising their children. I won't brag about our six grandchildren, except to state that they are wonderful.

Our Mexican workers have gained even more skill as nursery workers and their English has improved. Javier, who manages the greenhouses and can yard, has taken nursery related classes at the community college. Isidra and her husband have their own nursery, but she still works here and keeps everyone straight. Ernesto, who manages the field crew, brought his wife and two little boys from Mexico. They live in a mobile home here at the nursery. Since they have lived here, they have added two more babies to the family. The Mexican-American children of our workers are growing, and I can state unequivocally that they too are wonderful.

Now that you are up to date on all the main news from the tree farm, turn the pages and read the details.

Chapter 1
The Smells of Farmers

S ometimes when you live on a farm it is not desirable to have an acute sense of smell. Farm smells are something we have to live with. Then there are farmer smells.

I was born with a very good nose. It served me well when I was doing medical nursing. I could detect the odors of all sorts of conditions before the symptoms appeared. I was careful not to tell anyone. They would have thought I was crazy. Now however, physicians are beginning to acknowledge the value of the nose in making a diagnosis.

When I was seventeen and in love with a sailor, I would experience an erotic flashback if I passed a man who smelled like my sailor. It was a mixture of Lucky Strike cigarettes caught in the musty wool of blues that had been in the bottom of a sea bag. Now, I abhor the smell of cigarettes and don't care much for that sailor.

Lately my affectionate feelings are triggered by a different smell. My husband comes in from the fields at about ten to check in with our son who manages the office. Nice man that he is, he comes to where I am in the house and gives me a little hug. I bury my nose in the side of his neck, and in addition to his nice warm masculine smell, I smell diesel.

I don't know how it happens, but he manages to get tractor fuel on his hands and it gets transferred to other parts of his body.

He is an early riser and slips out of bed long before I am ready to begin my day. I always roll over to his side of the bed and, guess what, his pillow smells of diesel. He showers every night; maybe it is in his ears or hair.

Goodness! I hope I don't develop an erotic attachment to diesel fuel.

He also has a good nose. When I first met him, I was wearing the French perfume that I had worn since I was twenty. It is a spicy floral scent. He sniffed the air and said, "That perfume is wonderful. They preserved the smell of carnations exactly."

He went on to tell me that he had spent one summer at Oregon State University in a greenhouse, hybridizing carnations. Ever since it has been his favorite scent.

When we went to Paris a few years after we were married, he bought me two ounces of that perfume. I had been buying it in 7 1/2 cc bottles, so this was a wonderful luxury. It is hard to find, but one day I was in a discount store that buys from the overstock of department stores. I found my scent in a cologne and bought several bottles. When I told Verl, he went to the store and bought ten.

Verl can't quite duplicate the trick of the main character in the movie *Scent of a Woman*—identifying the name of every perfume he smells. But he can tell me what ingredients make up most of the common perfumes.

My love of scents goes back a long way. When I was twelve, my father told my mother to tell me—dads didn't tell daughters directly in those days—that I wore so much perfume that I smelled like a street walker.

I told this to my daughter and she said, "Oh, so you wore too much perfume then too." Daughters are like that these days.

Then she went on to say that Leslie, my teenaged granddaughter wanted to wear perfume so she would smell good, like grandma. Bless Leslie.

If you come to our house, and you have a good nose, you will smell a man who smells of diesel and a woman who smells like carnations.

Now, I've been wondering, do ranchers smell of cows, horses, and leather? Do the women in their lives become attached to those particular scents? Do the scents of mint or cauliflower permeate the clothes of the men who raise them? I remember that my grandfather smelled like wheat during threshing season and fresh hay after he fed the animals. Dare I ask about the people who raise pigs?

Perhaps the perfumeries are missing a market. I wonder if a shaving lotion called Western Farmer would sell.

Chapter 2
Barn or House, What's the Difference?

Twenty years ago when I married Verl and moved from Portland to the nursery, I discovered that I had forgotten a few things about farm life. One was that there is no separation between the farm and the farm house.

The two aren't as close, of course, as the farms in Switzerland where the barn is the first floor of the chalet. Or the farms in colonial New England where all the buildings are joined. But they are sometimes a little too close for me.

We do have a mud room and house rules about dirty boots. However, the office is in what used to be a back bedroom with a new outside entrance. I can't really expect the nurserymen to remove their shoes before they enter—or if they need to use the bathroom, or answer a ringing phone.

Evidence of the day's traffic is sprinkled down the back hall. A year ago we replaced the ugly orange and green flowered carpet with nice smooth ceramic tile. I just sigh and sweep up that good Willamette silty clay loam and dump it in the garbage. Maybe I should keep a pot nearby. Good soil shouldn't be wasted.

When we were married I found strange things in the refrigerator and bedroom. I pulled open the drawer at the bottom of the gun cabinet — a prenuptial gift from me to Verl — and pulled out some strange objects.

"What are these things for?" I asked my loving spouse.

"Caps, to set off dynamite."

You can guess how many seconds it took to have those things outside.

Then, I found the stuff that goes with the caps in the freezer! Verl said it keeps it from deteriorating. It also went outside in a hurry. He doesn't have any such material anymore, he says, not since the Mr. Bang fiasco that I wrote about in my first book. (Short synopsis: Blasted tree stump crashes through the roof of tenant house and skewers the waterbed. Big flood!)

Strange seeds appear in the refrigerator. Nurserymen are always collecting seeds. Other people travel and look at the sights. My husband and his buddies go on plant hunting expeditions. Sometimes the seeds are in there so long, he forgets what they are. Then they become mystery plants.

I was complaining—scratch that—discussing this with my good friend and columnist, Debbie Bixby. What she told me made me glad we don't raise animals. She said she was always suspicious of frozen meat she took from the freezer. It could be a specimen collected for the veterinarian, or an organ to be dissected at 4H, or even pelts the kids had saved for that tanning project.

Objects not only enter the house from the farm, but things disappear from the house and are swallowed up in the nursery. Things like tools. When I married Verl, I had been a single householder for twenty years and had a nice set of tools. They have disappeared, down to the shop, I hope. I now have an expensive brass set, hammer and screw drivers, that I bought at a gift shop. I keep them hidden in my office. Instead of trying to fix anything that requires more complicated tools, I turn the job over to Verl and let him search.

I've bought a dozen or so clippers over the years. I marked them with admonitions, in Spanish and English, saying they belonged to Florence, solamente. They disappeared anyway. Then I got smart and hunted up an old dull set. No one has stolen those.

My daughter Shevawn has left her career as a financial officer and started her own business, offering financial advice to small and medium sized companies. She works out of her home. Her office is in the master bedroom. Her three little boys have their own computer. Sometimes they disagree on which computer game they want to play or Louis, who is ten, has a report to do for school. Then Shevawn's domain is invaded. Perhaps my problem will soon be a universal one.

There are positives in having the farm and house close. I have lunch with my husband every day, and I almost always know where he is, within a hundred acres.

Chapter 3
Tractors

My husband collects tractors—not antiques although some are old—just tractors. Of course he denies this. He says he doesn't collect; he only buys what he needs. You be the judge.

We have one hundred and fifty acres under cultivation, spread across four farms. Trees and shrubs grow in the fields and ground covers are in the greenhouses or can yard. We employ fifteen people. Half spend their time propagating plants and working in the green houses or can yard and the other half work in the fields.

How then do we need twenty-four tractors—or is it twenty-eight now?

Several days ago, I was teasing my hardworking spouse about his addiction to possessing tractors. He said he needed them because there were such a variety of tasks that required a tractor, and it took too much time to change the equipment that was attached to them. I asked him to tell me what he used each of them for. He listed his equipment for me and told me why he needed it. It didn't all add up but you will get the idea.

First, he mentioned an International T. D. 6 Crawler, diesel with a wide track for soft ground. He bought this about ten years ago to operate the tree digger that was going to revolutionize our operation. But the tree digger didn't work in our sticky soil. It broke the root balls, endangering the survival of the tree, and he abandoned the idea. Now it is used occasionally when someone wants a very large tree. It is also good for pulling out vehicles that are mired in mud.

Next, he listed three John Deere Tractors. They have various implements attached. Two have front loaders. All are at least twenty years old. One of these is Verl's favorite tractor and he refers to it as *My Good Friend Johnny*.

Then there are the five old Allis-Chalmers, from the Forties and Fifties. They have been overhauled and are painted bright orange. They are the favorite vehicles of the field crew. The men are from one family whose home is a village in the mountains of Mexico. They are small, powerful men who work very hard. They sit atop these large orange vehicles as though they were kings.

Then there is the Ferrari, with the Lamborgini engine. It has four wheel drive and is thirty-three inches wide and articulated. This tractor is used in the vineyards of Europe. No one drives this tractor but Verl. He says it speaks only Italian and gutter English. The field crew speaks Spanish so....

We own eight Holders, all at least fifteen years old. Verl bought one and loved it. He calls it a baby Steiger, because of its 30 horse power. It also has four wheel drive, is articulated and thirty-three inches wide. It looks a little like an ant to me, and I guess it works like one too. It was manufactured in the Seventies. He says he bought two more because they worked so well. One is only twenty-four inches wide, the smallest commercial tractor ever made. It has been difficult to get parts for them. He has searched all over the states and Canada and has been in touch with the manufacturer in Germany, without much luck. So when he had a chance, he bought three more, to use for parts, he said. Instead he fixed them up. At the moment, six are running.

Then there is the little John Deere lawn mower tractor, with a Kawasaki air cooled engine, he tells me: "A great little machine."

Finally there are the two Kubotas. They were purchased in the 1980's and are thirty-three inches wide. They are used around the green houses to pull trailers to and from the planting machines. Our female workers like them. I look out and see Isidra, wearing a picture hat, happily driving a Kubota and looking exactly like the advertisement on television.

Verl didn't mention the five rototillers or the fork lift. He is very fond of trucks also.

When he sees an ad in the *Capital Press* for a tractor, his eyes flash green and he confesses that he just has to go and look at it. I'm sure if he likes it he will have a perfectly rational reason for buying it.

He is successful at his business and I confine my advice to personnel problems and major decisions. I don't fuss about the tractors. I just store the knowledge away, until I see something I just am dying to have, like a necklace, oriental rug, or computer. When I tell him about it, if he says, "My Gosh, Dear!" (Meaning: I'm shocked that you would think of spending so much on a nonessential.) I bring up the tractors and all objections cease.

Chapter 4
Where's Verl

You are familiar with the Where's Waldo books, I'm sure. Now substitute blue spruce trees for all those people in the Waldo cartoons, and look for one nurseryman, with gray hair and red suspenders. That is a task I perform at least once a week. Our workers do it even more often than I.

He might be anywhere on our four farms, out in the fields checking the trees for spider mites, noting if the crew fertilized every plant, taking cuttings for propagation, or in the shop down the road inventing some new farm implement. He might have gone to the tire store or lumber mill. Perhaps he is visiting the accountant or the lawyer. Wherever he is, between seven and five, you can be sure he is working.

He does tell someone when he takes his big truck, his favorite toy, to Seattle with a load. Since he is the only person on the nursery with a commercial truck driver's license, that is his task. He also likes to make that trip so that he can go to the customer's bank and cash the check. Several times, long ago. he was given worthless checks by Washington customers.

During the week, if he is expecting a customer to arrive, he tells Paul or Javier. On the weekend I hear, "I'm going over to Lardon Road. A buyer from the East is supposed to be here. Tell him....." Or it might be "a fellow who wants arbor-vitae" or "a man who wants to look at the Japanese maples."

However if he isn't expecting someone, he just disappears and is swallowed up by the green things he grows. I have bought bells to summon him, but one farm is fifteen miles away. I cultivated a call, modeled after the one my grandmother used when she would intone, "Floss-EEEEE!" across the farm. But my "Ver-EEEELLLL!" doesn't seem to carry as far. I might try driving around and looking for him. However, I don't like to drive the pick-up trucks that are parked here and there. The inside is usually covered with an inch of dust and the driver should have an intimate knowledge of each vehicle. My van is too new and clean to subject it to the lanes on our places.

Verl had a portable phone that he carried for a while. The employees gave him a leather case for it as a birthday gift. It was embossed with his name and attached to his belt. He did wear it for a while when it was new. But then he forgot to recharge it and after a time, when it needed to be repaired, it got lost among the tools in the shop.

We hired a man who had been in the Army. He had the wonderful idea that radios would keep everyone in touch with everyone else. You know, "Ten four, over and out," and the rest of the calls we hear on T.V. The radios were heavy, but the Mexican employees wore them proudly because the wearer was designated as the crew chief for the particular job they were doing. I must confess that I never mastered the art of using the radio. I do have a doctorate and can use a computer, so I can't be completely stupid. Perhaps it was because I could never find one of these status objects. Someone was wearing it on his hip.

The workers would call Verl and then discover that his radio was in the outside office, under a layer of dust. He didn't need any status and the darn things were heavy. In time the radios went the way of the telephone. The man who suggested the radios is also gone.

I've tried the psychological approach. At strategic relaxed moments I've asked, "Did you resent your mother when she asked you where you were going?" Or, "Did Alice (first wife) keep pretty close track of where you were?"

Verl answers with a surprised tone, "No, I don't think so. They never asked."

So much for that approach.

Paul, Verl's son, has joined the business. When I want to know where Verl is, I go to the office where Paul spends much of his time and ask, "Where is your Dad?" Sometimes he knows, but often he doesn't. Then we smile and shake our heads. We both know and love Verl, even if we can never find him.

Chapter 5
The Royal Bed

A few years ago after a leisurely lunch, my good friend, Sally and I went antique shopping. Sally is also the wife of a nurseryman. Perhaps looking would be a better word since we seldom bought anything. Most men don't understand, but nothing is more relaxing for a woman than wandering through stores with a good friend, looking and commenting.

We strolled through a large antique store in Aurora, making remarks.

"Gee, Mom was so glad to get rid of Grandma's old library table, and now look what it is worth."

"You have a cut glass vase just like this one don't you?"

"Would you look at the price on this?"

We pulled up short and were struck dumb when we saw the bed. It had four thick carved walnut posts, each a foot in diameter and seven feet tall. There were rails between the posts for a canopy. The headboard was seven feet high and it was as large as a modern queen sized bed. As I looked at it I had visions of Hampton Court, Tom Jones, and Scarlet O'Hara.

A sales person joined Sally and me. "It is beautiful, isn't it? We just got it in. It came from New Orleans and was made about 1830."

"How much is it?" I asked in an awestruck voice.

"Let's see. I think it is fourteen hundred dollars."

Now this was a few years ago, perhaps ten— time goes so quickly as you get older—and that was a lot of money, but not impossible. I had a nice cherry four poster, but this was a dream bed. I wanted it—bad—but I decided to include Verl in the decision.

I went home and described the bed in glowing terms, the posts, the canopy and the beautiful wood. My nice husband could see that I lusted for this antique.

"Let's go and look at it and we'll see," he said. That meant yes.

It was Friday. Verl had a full day planned on Saturday, but we would go up in the late afternoon. We were there before five, but the store was closed. I led him around the side of the antique store and we peered through the window and the shadows at my dream bed.

Sunday we went to church. Wouldn't you know, it was pledge Sunday. The minister stood at the pulpit and extolled the virtues of tithing. And one female sinner sat in the congregation filled with sinful desire for a material object. I couldn't even think about the starving children in Africa, or the injustices The International Council of Churches would remedy.

It was a twenty mile drive to the antique store. On the way, Verl told me that the bed was a little intimidating for him. "I'll need a bedside table to hold my crown when I take it off at night." Then we speculated what various relatives would have to say about our royal couch.

Finally we were at the store and walked in, trying to appear as casual as we could. Perhaps we could bargain a bit.

We stood before the bed. "Well, it certainly is beautiful," said my dear husband. I was dizzy with excitement.

The owner strolled over. "Beautiful antique."

"Yes," I responded, coolly, "how much are you asking for it?"

"I'm not sure I want to sell it, but I'd let it go for fourteen thousand dollars."

"It certainly is lovely. Thank you," I said as we turned and left the store.

We didn't talk until we were almost home. Then we speculated about what would have happened if I had bought it the first day. Obviously the first salesman had made a mistake. Would we have gotten it out of the store before someone realized that one zero was missing from the check?

Of course I was disappointed, but surprisingly little. Whether I slept in my nice cherry four-poster, or in a kingly bed, made no real difference in my life. By the time we turned into the driveway, we were giggling about the whole episode.

A few years later, I decided that our double bed was too small for us. The togetherness was fine, but Verl's high body heat made sleeping difficult.

I was visiting a friend in North Carolina and we went to her son-in-law's fine furniture store, just to look. I saw a queen sized pencil post bed, designed by a Southern artist, a gentleman who lives in a restored log barn. I loved it and the price was right. I bought it and they shipped it to Oregon.

Instead of a bed fit for a king or plantation owner, we sleep in one that would fit right in a log cabin or a saltbox house. It suits us much better than the royal bed. But I still wonder what would have happened if I had bought *The Bed* at the first price mentioned.

Chapter 6
A Snow Story

When I interviewed for a job in Portland, the chairman of the Psychiatric Nursing Department made sure I saw the beauty of Oregon. I was driven around the city and up the Gorge to Multnomah Falls. We had dinner at Hood River in a restaurant overlooking the Columbia. I enjoyed it thoroughly but it wasn't really necessary. I had left upstate New York in a blinding St. Patrick's Day snow storm. When I arrived in Portland, the daffodils and camellias were blooming. One look and a sniff and I was instantly convinced that Oregon would be a wonderful place to live.

In the trips around the city, we passed the park blocks. I said, "Gee what a great place to use cross country skis." In New York, I was accustomed to putting on my skis on in the kitchen and poling out the back door for a jaunt through the winter woods and streets.

My hosts smiled at each other and told me that it didn't snow often in Portland.

In spite of the lack of access for cross country skiing, I wasn't sorry. All of my previous working life involved winter driving, early in the morning and late at night. Although I was a skilled snow driver, I would be glad to have no practice.

In Pennsylvania and Ohio where I had lived earlier, the snow came and went. It seldom was on the ground longer than two weeks. A warm spell would arrive and the dirty snow and slush would disappear. But upstate New York was another matter. The snow that fell in November was still there in April. The parking lot at Russell Sage College, the school where I taught, was large in October, but by Spring, the mountain of snow piled up by the snow plows had reduced the parking space considerably.

Troy, New York is an old city, the center of which was filled with lovely row houses built in the last century. There were no garages, of course, and the owners parked at the curb in front of their houses. To indicate that the space was a home owner's territory, an old kitchen chair was placed in the empty space. Woe be it to any stranger who moved the chair and parked in that spot.

I lived a few miles south of Troy in the town of East Greenbush. My house had a garage in the basement, which meant that I had a steep driveway. I had a contract with Rapid Snow Removal. The agreement was that I would be able to drive out of my driveway every morning at seven. The company lived up to its agreement, often arriving in the middle of the night to plow my exit to the road. They charged me by the inch and often their bill was as high as my utility bill.

With conditions like this, you can understand why it was not unusual for a winter bound person to burst into tears at the sight of the first crocus. Or why the daffodils figured more prominently in my decision to come to Portland than the salary offer.

But I do miss the snow stories. Each winter, we commuters would gather around someone's fireplace, sip hot chocolate and exchange snow stories with our fellow travelers. We would embroider them and exaggerate as much as we dared. Here in the Willamette Valley we have only ice storm stories, and since these storms are rare, and no one ventures out, they don't make for good tall tale telling.

When I was working at the Oregon Health Sciences University I did research in Union County, a beautiful area of Eastern Oregon. The warming effects of the Japanese current aren't felt there and it is as cold in the winter as any place in the United States. I was exploring the lives and problems of women in this county which could be classified frontier as well as rural.

Every woman I spoke with talked about of the difficulties caused by the isolation. Union County lies in a bowl ringed by mountains. The passes are high — the one to Pendleton is more than four thousand feet — and are often closed in the winter. Along with tales of winter blues, I collected some marvelous winter driving stories. The following story is my favorite.

The man in the family was a wheat farmer and the farm was one he inherited from his father. Still, if he wanted to pay for the new tractor— the huge expensive one— before it became an antique, he would have to earn money away from the farm. He found the perfect off-season job, working with the winter road crews that plowed the roads and spread sand on them.

He should have been called in the middle of the night when it first began to snow. Maybe it hadn't happened because the snow wasn't all that deep. But about dawn it began to blow and huge drifts were formed in less than an hour.

The dispatcher called him and he hopped out of bed, warmed up left over coffee in the microwave, and pulled on his warmest clothes. The four wheel drive pickup started without problems and he headed down the road to drive twenty miles to the highway garage. The snow didn't seem so deep and he had no trouble the first few miles.

But suddenly he was faced with a horrendous drift. It was eight feet deep and he guessed a hundred feet long.

There was no way he could get through it. He climbed out of his truck and stood watching the wind-whipped wall of snow build. Then he saw lights at the other end of the drift. A vehicle was parked there.

He called across and introduced himself. The person on the other side was a doctor who had the poor judgment to spend the weekend before in a mountain cabin. He was trying to get back to La Grande and his practice. The two men exchanged a few sentences and then each of them began to swim and dig through the deep snow. They met in the middle and exchanged keys. The last half of their struggle was easier because they were in the tracks of the other.

Then they stamped their feet, brushed the snow off their clothes, and climbed into the borrowed vehicles. They turned around carefully and continued on to their destinations. They met several days later and returned the automobiles.

I'm not sure why this is my favorite snow story. Perhaps it is because it tells something about Oregonians.

Chapter 7
Tight Squeeze

I inherited small light bones--the kind that look good on petite people. But I also inherited some other genes--the genes that enabled my Irish ancestors to survive the potato famine. I thrive on very little food and store fat easily. When I was a teenager my father told my mother, "Flossie is going to be heavy. She is built just like my mother".

I spent years proving him wrong. It wasn't so hard when I was doing general nursing and rushing up and down the ward each day for twenty miles or so. It got harder when I became a psychiatric nurse, an occupation that requires patience and intelligence, but not much physical effort. The years didn't make it easier either.

I hung on, dieting and exercising, and until I reached my sixth decade, I was reasonably thin. Then I said. "Enough. I have been hungry most of my life. I don't care anymore. I am going to stop dieting. "

As the result, I have now moved beyond plump to slightly obese.

But a few years ago, on the ferry between Victoria and Port Angeles, I had an experience that shook my resolve to eat, drink and enjoy life.

The ferry was crowded, and we were among the last cars to get on. We parked and then my husband, step-son, daughter-in-law, and I squeezed out the side door of the van while people parked the very last cars. We went up the stairs to the decks to relax and enjoy the breeze and beautiful sunset.

When the loudspeaker announced that it was time to return to the cars, I rushed down the stairs, followed at a distance by my husband who insisted that we had plenty of time.

When I got down to the deck where the cars were loaded, I saw that in our section they were parked a few inches apart. I tried one route after another through the sea of automobiles, only to be frustrated by immovable rear view mirrors that were the same height as a wide portion of my anatomy. I couldn't get through to our van.

The cars around me filled up with children and skinny tourists. Then my husband called across the vehicles, "Get in the car. They'll be moving soon."

Where had he been? Everyone looked. "I can't get through. Here are the keys." I threw them to him. The kids had made it, I saw.

"I climbed over that pick-up," said my helpful spouse.

I approached that vehicle. Three teen-aged boys said, "We'll help you."

I was wearing a new black cotton dress — a little short but stylish. I didn't fancy struggling over that truck with an audience. So I politely declined and began rushing between cars, measuring my anatomy against the spaces between rear view mirrors and muddy cars six inches away.

One helpful gentleman said, "I'd move my mirror for you if I could."

People called suggestions, "Jump!", "Duck down!"

I get bigger when I squat.

The Japanese tourists in a van smiled and nodded their heads encouragingly.

In desperation, I pressed my back against a car, threw back my shoulders, stood on my tip toes, and rolled the lower part of my rib cage (33 inches in circumference) through a four inch space. My dress cleaned the road grime off both cars.

But I made it.

The Japanese tourists clapped and the people in the other cars cheered. I slipped into our van and tried to appear small.

Was I embarrassed? I should have been. But no one was laughing at me. They were all encouraging me and trying to help.

I did resolve to go on a diet but by the next morning the resolve had vanished. Next time I have to get on a ferry, I'll make sure we get there very early so that we can park with a little extra space.

I promised myself that if I ever saw a large person in a situation such as the one I just experienced, I wouldn't laugh — at least in her presence.

Chapter 8
What the Kids Leave Behind

The day finally arrives and the kids leave home. This event can be a reason to celebrate or an occasion for tears. I suspect that for most parents it is a little of each.

Freud wrote about this period in the mother's life. (He never mentioned the father.) He wrote about the empty nest and described women who lost their life role and developed involutional melancholia. But Freud is outdated. I hear expressions of relief when I talk to my friends, relief that the loud rock music is gone, and a roast lasts more than one meal. The sadness comes later, when time and life experience (and maybe a little of your early influence) turn your children into really nice people — and they live too far away for you to see them as much as you'd like.

It is interesting to note what young people take with them when they leave home, and what they leave behind. They take the best car they can drive away, their stereo and tapes, and the clothes they're wearing this year. Last year's clothes stay in your closet. My daughters also borrowed all of my household tools, the hammer, screwdrivers, etc. They took the antiques my mother had left them and a few that she left to me. And of course the kids take all the old furniture from the attic to furnish their first apartment.

What don't they take? One thing they are sure to leave behind is their pets. I have done a little informal research on this and my data shows that 99.9 % of college graduates leave their pets behind when they move into their first residence. No matter how much they profess to love old Spot, or Scratchy Kitty, they leave him behind with their parents.

When my older daughter, Susan, was married, one of the couple's *thoughtful* friends gave them a gift, a large male German shepherd. They were grateful for the gift, in spite of the fact that they were moving into a pet-free apartment. They just shipped the animal off to the farm of my son-in-law's parents, where he lived out his days and died of old age.

My step-son, Paul, left his hunting dog, Rusty, behind when he moved into his own place. He acquired another dog, but Rusty remained ours. You could always tell when Paul drove in because of the delighted yelps from Rusty's pen.

Kristi, my step-daughter, left her two cats here when she moved to Boston three years ago. She is back in Portland, but the felines are still with us.

A friend tells me that she has a boat in her garage that belongs to her son. Another had a rusty old Ford parked in the machine shed that her son thinks he'll restore someday. Kristi's prize antique sofa, the funky one she bought for fifteen dollars, is stored in our barn. An old seal coat that one daughter bought at a rummage sale for five dollars graced my closet for fifteen years.

There are text books for courses I never took in my bookcases and two volumes of poetry that are stamped Cleveland Heights Public Library.

The things I've mentioned are all belongings we parents wish the children would take with them. There are other things that we'd like to keep.

I have the my daughter's report cards carefully filed away. My step children's reports are taped to the inside of a cupboard door in my study. My husband put them there years ago, and they are yellow with age. I had my younger daughter's girl scout sash, the one with thirty-six merit badges sewn on with big stitches. I kept it until her son joined the Cub Scouts and then mailed it to her.

I have the post cards sent from Girl Scout Camp. I gave my daughters fourteen stamped and addressed post-cards when I kissed them good-bye. Their accounts of camp are hilarious — long lists of disasters, ending with, "I am having a wonderful time, Love." Maybe I'll give them to my grandchildren someday.

My shelves are crowded with photo albums full of pictures of my dear little girls, and now their children. Forty plus Christmases and ten graduations are enclosed in those albums.

Perhaps we parents shouldn't be so hard on our grown children when they force us to assume guardian-ship of their pets and possessions. Perhaps they are leav-ing a little of themselves with us when they move into adult-hood. I try to be understanding. But occasionally I have fantasies. Wouldn't it be fun to sell everything, buy an R.V, and tell the kids to come and pick up their stuff?

Chapter 9
Seasonal Diseases

My husband has a happy temperament. Generally he is enthusiastic about the plants he grows, pleased with the status of our nursery business, and full of plans for the future. He is easy to live with. But every year, beginning in February I notice the symptoms of a seasonal disease. He'll sigh deeply and deliver pronouncements like, "I don't know how long we can stay in the nursery business."

Alarmed I go through the clarifying questions — I have been a psychotherapist : "Are orders down this year?"; "Did one of your big customers cancel?"; "Did the trees you just grafted die?"

He answers, "No," to all my questions. Then the cause of this sad mood hits me. Tax time is approaching and my usually happy spouse has that painful condition known as ta*xitis.*

Now I have never suffered this disease. I have always worked for hospitals and schools. Every month my paycheck arrived and I looked at the net amount and planned my budget based on it. Oh, I did start to look at the deductions after one of my colleagues had to pay a large sum because the pay roll clerk had made an error and did not deduct enough income tax. But generally I considered taxes something like Western Oregon rain, inconvenient at times, but necessary and of considerable benefit.

My spouse, however, considers all the money that comes in to be his, earned by his blood and sweat. When Uncle Sam or Oregon State demands some of it, it is a painful operation. I try to restore balance and reality, because I don't want him to make any decisions when he is in a depressed state caused by taxitis.

Every other year he is afflicted with another disease as well. He sits down at lunch, with his mail, picks up the legislative bulletin and says, "Look what they are trying to do to us now?" Then he reads off the list of proposed bills. When he gets to the bills about water, he turns a dusky color. He is suffering from legislative paranoia.

Again, I trot out my clarifying responses: "Those are just proposals, aren't they?" "That is so far out it isn't likely to pass, is it?" "Have you called our legislator?"

New OHSA regulations and changes in the immigration laws also produce symptoms. They aren't seasonal. You never know when these maladies will hit.

Sometimes it takes all my skill to restore my nice husband to a minimal degree of functioning. The other day, I was tired and suffering from my own symptoms brought on by poor book sales. I didn't have the energy to attempt to restore my husband's good humor. So I tried to use a technique called paradoxical instruction. This is where you agree with your patient's delusions, and tell him in an exaggerated way, to do what you don't want him to do. You hope he will do the opposite which is what you really want. I don't use this technique with patients because it is dishonest. However it does work. Parents use it often with their kids — " So you want to run away, Sonny. Let me pack your bag."

So in solemn tones I said, "We can't even sell the business, no one has the money to buy it. We can probably live on my pension, if we eat only oatmeal and skip movies.

Maybe we could move in with the kids." Then I sobbed and blew my nose. You get the idea.

And you know what? I looked across the table and my husband's green eyes were sparkling. He was laughing at me. And for that day at least he had a remission in his taxitis and legislative maladies.

Now what am I going to try the next time the symptoms return?

Chapter 10
The Mystery of the Pink Herons

I didn't notice the pink herons when we first arrived home from vacation. There were too many other pressing problems.

First there was the flood in the garage. We saw evidence that things had been awash there as we stepped out of the van. Javier, the employee in charge during our absence rushed in to tell my husband that the gauge on the house water pump had broken. He had shut off the water to the house. Verl and Javier hurried out to the irrigation well to switch water valves.

I unlocked the door, shut off the alarm and was greeted by a meow. Mommy Cat was in the house.

All of our dozen cats are outside cats. (They are all neutered, so please, no lectures.) But Mommy must have been someone's house cat before she arrived at our door, ten years ago, with four kittens. She dashes into the house when the door is opened, and then hides. She must have come in when we took our suitcases to the van, five days before.

She had plenty of food. There was an open twenty pound sack of cat food in the utility room. She jumped up on the sink and drank from the breakfast dishes I'd left soaking in the sink.

Now the question was, what did she use for a litter box?

She picked the spot that most resembled the lawn, the lush pile of one of my favorite possessions, my deep blue Chinese rug. There were five little piles there, well dried, and partially covered with the wool she had scratched up from the rug. There were only two damp spots—poor Mommy had been dehydrated. She thoughtfully voided on the pink flowers at the edge of the rug, so the blue wasn't stained.

I cleaned up the mess, ran the sweeper and sponged the damp spots. And guess what? The rug looked like new. There is something to be said for well-made wool rugs.

But I didn't make my usual post vacation outside inspection. So I missed seeing the herons until several days later.

When we were first married, my husband asked a Silverton artist, Norman Brendan, to make a sculpture for a pond in the front of our house. It is landscaped as a Japanese garden.

Norm welded a pair of herons from strips of steel. They are a favorite possession. There is a romantic quality to the piece. One bird stands protectively over the other which has a feminine stance. The steel was supposed to rust, and give an interesting finish.

They have remained beautiful. However the pond has had problems. In spite of all our efforts it leaks. In fact it is now dry.

When we went on vacation, it was filled with pine needles. It was still an interesting sight, with the herons, the stone edges and a weeping blue atlas cedar trailing its branches over the pond, like the robes of an ancient crone.

A few days after we returned, I went out the front door, as I said good by to Kristi, our daughter, and looked in the direction of my beloved herons.

Horrors, they had been painted pink! With blue eyes!

Kristi almost collapsed on the walk, weak with laughter.

The pond had been swept clean and pink enamel carefully applied to my sculpture.

Was it vandalism? No, no person bent on destruction would take such care.

Was someone making a joke? No one I know sophisticated enough to plan such a joke would damage a work of art to carry it out.

I knew who had done it. One of our employees. They have a practice of welcoming my husband and me when we return from a trip by doing something nice. One time they weeded my flower bed and bark dusted it. Another time they organized the nursery to a state of neatness never before seen. This time someone had turned our rusty herons into pretty pink flamingos.

Now what am I going to do? Do I go out and in my halting Spanish ask who painted my birds?

And then, when I get a reply, do I say, "Thank you"? I can't very well say, "You ruined a valuable piece of art" especially when someone had bought enamel and carefully painted the feathers.

I should be upset, but every time I think of my pink herons, I smile. I could pontificate about the relativity of art and beauty, but I won't. I know exactly the feeling my mother had when she said, "I'm so tickled." And that is enough.

Chapter 11
Los Guajolotes (The Turkeys)

A few years ago I took a walk to what my husband calls *the back forty*. It was a wonderful early fall evening.I stopped by our pond, admired the ducks, looked for a heron and listened to the frogs. Then I followed the footprints of one of our resident deer to the arbor-vitae where he grooms his horns. He has ruined the tree, but since he uses the same tree, it is a small loss and our contribution to wildlife. In the dust on the ground I saw the tracks of our quail family, but wait, there were larger tracks as well.

And then I saw them — six black and white turkeys. They were picking at weeds and blackberries at the edge of the field. They didn't fly when I approached. They just walked away with a dignified gait. I was half a mile from my house and even farther from buildings on the adjoining farms. Where had they come from?

When I came back to our out buildings, I met one of our workers who was working late. I'll call him Juan Doe, for reasons that will become evident.

"Juan, guess what I just saw? Six big turkeys, back across the pond."

"Six? There were ten. We had company last weekend and we cooked two. They tasted good."

I guess they don't have rules about a neighbor's livestock in Mexico.

"Gosh, Juan. They might belong to someoné. We'd better not kill any more."

"Okay, Florence."

I wondered what happened to the missing two. Food for the fox that lives in the woods, perhaps.

I told my husband about the birds and we began to ask neighbors if they had lost turkeys. Then my stepson, Paul, went down the lane on the three wheeler, located the birds and herded them up to the vacant dog pen. We made a trip to Wilco and got a big bag of turkey feed.

The first night they flew out of the pen and roosted in the trees, returning in the morning to eat. We covered the top of the pen and confined them.

I began to go out every day to say hello. "Gobble, Gobble." The employees stopped by to greet the birds, and Isidra brought her children, Carmen and Louis, over to see them.

I began to get worried. I would never be able to eat them. I like meat and eat it almost daily, but I prefer to think it comes from the supermarket or the freezer. I loved lamb, until we got a few sheep, and since then my throat rebels and I can't swallow it. I know, it's irrational. It is not anti-agricultural, however. My grandfather, who had a large successful Pennsylvania farm always left home for a few days when the animals were slaughtered. He evidently liked to think that meat came from the smoke house.

About a week later, my husband came home from the local fruit stand with some news. The man who runs the stand asked if he had seen any turkeys.

"Yes. We found six and shut them up. Are they yours?"

"Heck, no. The fish and wild life people brought them from Texas to stock the woods. They let a bunch loose, but no one has seen them."

'Oops, here we were harboring wild birds that were protected. So Paul opened the pen and herded our pets back down the lane and into the field.

I informed Juan Doe that the birds were protected by the government and weren't to be bothered.

"Si. I don't want no trouble."

We kept looking for them when we were at the back of the property. I worried that the six would go the way of the missing two. One night at three A.M. when we awoke together my husband mumbled, "I wonder where the turkeys are roosting?"

A few days later, I came home from Spanish class and pulled into the driveway. There in the front yard were the turkeys. Our cats were eyeing these invaders with interest. A while later someone put some turkey feed out and they had a feast. They tried out my wrought iron patio furniture as roosts but they disappeared at dusk.

Next day they were back, practicing mating in the driveway while a truck was being loaded. They marched around the house, picking up seeds, going back into their pen, and greeting the workers with a Spanish gobble. My step-daughter, Kristi, is a photographer and the turkeys became her subjects.

One flew down from the roof of a greenhouse, landing on the windshield of the car of one of our employees. The windshield shattered and the poor turkey died. The others began to roost on the employees' cars and our tractors.

We had to do something about these unwanted pets. One night after dark, Verl crept into the dog pen with sacks and captured them. We put them into the trunk of the car and drove them to our friends, Dick and Sally. They love birds and when they lived in California they had a pet turkey that had a role in a movie. They were excited to hear that they were going to have some turkeys to add to their flocks of geese, ducks and swans.

We drove into our friend's garage and closed the door. There was furious gobbling when we opened the sacks and Tom and his harem emerged. One feathered lady flew toward me and perched for a time atop my head. Thank goodness I was wearing a hat.

Several years later, Tom is still alive. Unfortunately, the ladies laid their eggs and nested on the ground. They probably provided meals for the resident foxes and coyotes. Sally even brought in a several domestic ladies to keep Tom happy but they soon met the same fate as their wild sisters.

So much for wild Texas turkeys.

Chapter 12
Laurel and Hardy, on the Farm

Did you ever feel as though you had been dropped into the middle of a scene from a Laurel and Hardy movie? I seem to have that sort of experience often.

The most recent episode of *Florence and Verl Face Life* began when I walked into the dark kitchen and heard an ominous plopping drip. I turned on the light. Yes, the roof was leaking—again. A steady drip was falling from a beam onto the kitchen counter. I got out the roasting pan, put it under the drip, and added an old tea towel to reduce the spatter.

Those of you who have read my first book know about the roof. The plan for our house was an architecture student's master's thesis. It was built thirty-five years ago and is still very modern with lots of glass and open space. But the roof has always been a problem. It is almost flat, resembling a squashed M. The valley between the hills is a stream when it rains and most of the leaks have originated there. Several years ago, my husband and a carpenter friend built a cricket in the gully, supposedly solving the problem.

"The roof is leaking, " I announced to my spouse.

"I'll fix it when it stops raining. Anyway, I'm too busy now." He went on to enumerate the tasks that were more important than keeping the rain out of the kitchen. It was shipping season, the busiest time of the year at the nursery.

Three days passed. The drip was not clean rain water, but dirty brown stuff.

Saturday morning I awakened to the sound of footsteps on the roof. Great, the roof was being fixed. I got up, put on the wine red velvet robe my daughter had sent as a gift and tried my new bejeweled slippers. An intact roof is cause for celebration. Then I settled down at the kitchen table with a pot of tea and the paper.

The steps continued and there was also the sound of the high pressure hose but I sipped, read and enjoyed my morning. Then debris began flying against the kitchen window—and sticking. I went to the sliding glass door that leads to the patio to tell Verl to rinse off the window, but there was too much water spraying around for me to open the door.

I returned to the paper. Soon the window was being sprayed with clean water. Nice, I thought. Then the wand of the hose began tapping against the window—a signal.

I went back to the door, and looked out at bedlam. The hose was on the ground, flopping around like a hyperactive snake, spraying water, bark dust and cat food all over the patio. The ladder to the roof was on the ground. I looked up and saw my nice husband waving his arms. His face was red and his mouth was moving, but the noise of the hose's motor obscured the words.

I dashed out. He was motioning toward the ladder but my first priority was to stop the water. But where was the darn switch? My feet were plastered with bark dust and water dribbled down my back. He was yelling directions but where was the switch?

I abandoned the sprayer and went for the wand. At least I could direct the water until I got the darn thing turned off.

Antonio, our faithful worker, came loping across the lawn. He also had trouble locating the switch, but finally found it. Just as the motor ceased, I heard my husband's voice saying something about low I.Q.'s. Antonio put the ladder back against the roof and ran back to the head propagation house. Antonio knows when to avoid the boss.

I looked around at the patio and said, "What a mess!"

As Verl climbed down he said, "I'm too busy to clean it up."

I went into the house, washed my feet and put on blue jeans and a sweat shirt. Saks Fifth Avenue robes and fancy slippers don't do it around here.

I decided not to mention the remark about my intelligence. We have a good marriage and I don't let minor things upset me. That night at dinner, however, I was tempted. My husband said, "I need to take you around the nursery and show you how to shut off all the machinery."

"Fine, I really should know that." I thought of offering to show him how to use the word processing program, the CD player, and the VCR, but I'll wait until a better time.

The drip has slowed. Evidently the water was dammed up by the cricket but it should be empty soon. The ladder is still in place. The cats have been using it as a jungle gym. It is probably wise to leave it there since more work may need to be done.

If we didn't have the roof, we wouldn't have so much to laugh about.

Chapter 13
Boys Have More Fun

When I've reminisced about our growing up with my brother, John, or shared childhood secrets with my husband, Verl, I've learned that boys have more fun. They have better stories about the adventures of their tender years.

I've been tempted to write a series of stories about Rowdy and Johnny. Verl's grandfather called him Rowdy. They would be great stories, but I'm afraid they should be read only by adults. They might give kids bad ideas.

My adventures that are worth repeating seem to have taken place when I was with my brother. Like the time we went hunting with my great-grand father's double barreled muzzle loaded gun. It kicked so hard you had to lean against a tree when you fired it.

I saw a rabbit, found a tree, and aimed. I ended up with a bloody nose and the hare escaped. That is the last time I've been hunting. Do you suppose my brother planned it that way?

Rowdy grew up in Northern Idaho and Johnny in Western Pennsylvania. Yet their stories are remarkably similar.

Rowdy tells about filling his trouser legs with dry soil and putting rubber bands around his ankles. Then he and his friends would race each other. The object was not to cross the finish line but to see who could make the most dust. (His mother didn't have a washing machine.)

There was an odor of revenge about Johnny's pranks. If an adult was mean to the boys, they might live to regret it. Old man Kerr was nasty. He chased the boys when they went by on their bikes and swore at them if they paused to rest under his apple tree.

On Halloween his outhouse was a favorite target. Not content to dump it on its side, one year the boys put it on his porch. The next fall Mr. Kerr swore to put an end to such behavior. He seated himself in the little building at dark, with his loaded shotgun across his knees.

Johnny, Harold and Goodman saw him go in. They amused themselves with other pursuits and let him get cold and tired. Then they quietly sneaked up behind and pushed the outhouse over on its door, trapping the irate old man.

There was a casualty however. Goodman, a handsome Swedish boy, slipped and fell into the pit. Covered with Mr. Kerr's ———— , he begged his cohorts to give him a hand. When they hesitated to grasp his dripping hand, he swore in Swedish and crawled out. He ran a quarter of a mile down the steep hill to the creek and jumped in. Creeks in Pennsylvania are very cold in late October.

After that, Mr. Kerr and the boys called a truce. It wasn't long before all three of the boys were drafted and sent overseas.

Many of Rowdy's stories involve his battle with the old horse he rode when he spent his summers herding sheep. At every opportunity, it bit him, brushed him off with tree limbs, and scratched his legs along fences. Maybe that is why he is so attached to tractors or anything else that has a motor.

It must be something in the male genes. My grandfather, even as a young married man, had a great time on

Halloween. His favorite story was about putting his neighbor's wagon on top of the barn. I've read that the students at M.I.T. put a V.W. bug on the roof of a dormitory.

I preferred to get my adventures second hand, while seated safely in a chair. I read books like *Captain Blood* , *The Count of Monte Cristo* , and *Tom Sawyer* while my brother was out pushing over outhouses. I like the way I found adventure, but his way does make entertaining reading.

Chapter 14
Mr. Fix It

I t is very convenient to have a husband (or wife) who can make minor and major repairs around the house. Verl is a good electrician, a passable plumber and a good enough carpenter. And since he works on this farm or at one of our nearby farms, he is always available.

Well, you'd think he would be, wouldn't you?

The toilet in my bathroom had been emitting glug glug sounds for a year. Then a few months ago it began to run constantly. No amount of jiggling or tinkering with the mechanism in the tank did the job.

One day I announced, "You have got to fix the toilet."

"Yes, Dear," said my sweet husband.

One morning I got up, staggered in my half asleep state to the bathroom, and discovered that the toilet wouldn't flush. I waited until my early bird husband checked in for phone messages about ten.

"My toilet won't flush. When on earth are you going to fix it ? "

"Oh, I forgot to tell you. It kept me awake running last night. I got up and shut it off." He hurried in to turn the valve, anything to get away from the explosion that was about to occur in the kitchen.

The faucet in the kitchen had been strange for several years. The mechanism that turns on the water is one arm that swings to the left for hot water and to the right for cold. It wouldn't shut off when it was in the hot position. I had adapted to this peculiarity but the cleaning lady and any guests might be faced with a rush of hot water that they couldn't control. The sprayer had also stopped working. Verl promised to fix it, but said that we had to go together to pick out the faucet, a trip that was postponed regularly.

Finally I hit upon a strategy better than nagging or threatening to go on strike. I said, "Who is the best plumber in Silverton? I am going to call him to fix the toilet and faucet?"

"No, No, I'll do it. My manhood couldn't stand to see a professional do my job." His green eyes were merry.

"When?" I was steely eyed and stern.

"Thursday, we'll go to the plumbing supply store and you pick out the faucet."

And we did go. I was very impressed with the female sales clerks, who apparently knew everything about plumbing. Verl discussed everything with the woman who helped him and I trotted along behind. He picked out the faucet, but I had no objection to his choice.

The following Saturday he disappeared into my bathroom with thirty pounds of tools. My bathroom is just off our bedroom. I had banished Verl to the other bathroom as soon as Paul left home. His shows the signs that a very busy farmer with muddy boots dashes in regularly. Mine is a ladies bath. I did hate to entrust my lovely private room to that farmer with his big wrenches, but I did.

Several hours later, my bathroom looked like his, but my toilet worked. We admired it together and I mentioned it gratefully every ten minutes for the rest of the weekend. On Monday I showed it to his mother when she dropped over. I didn't study experimental psychology for nothing. I knew that behavior that is positively reinforced is more likely to be repeated.

On Sunday morning I sat in the breakfast room drinking my Sunday pot of tea and reading the Sunday paper. This is one of the distinct pleasures of retirement. Verl came trundling in, with his three foot long monkey wrench and an arm load of assorted tools. He was ready to fix the faucet.

I decided not to watch and kept my eyes glued to the paper. It was a hard thing to do. Unable to contain myself, as I listened to the bang, bang of heavy steel tools on delicate tile, I said, "Please be careful when you put the tools on the floor. Remember it is ceramic."

"I'm being careful," grunt, "Dear."

It was too much. I got up and glanced across the counter and there was the sink, sitting on the floor. I fled to the bedroom, dressed and then hid in my study.

The banging and grunting went on. Soon there was a chorus of curses. I had never heard my husband swear like that. Oh, he might say, G___D___, but never a string of deeply felt emotional curses directed at the plumbing under the sink. In fact, I haven't heard anyone swear like that since my father died. I was grateful that it was good old fashioned swearing, not the Eddie Murphy type that one hears now days. But still it was frightening.

I went into the kitchen to see if I could help. Now the garbage disposal sat in the floor beside the sink.

"Are you all right, Honey?" I was cautious. I didn't know if his anger was global.

He got up quickly from the floor, gave me a little kiss and said, "This job is more difficult than I thought. I have to go to the store and get some things."

He went to the store, and to our shop. In between, the swearing continued and I stayed in my study and tried to ignore it. I was grateful that he didn't want me there holding tools, a service that my father had always insisted that my mother perform.

Finally about four, I heard the sound of the broom and ventured into the kitchen. The sink was back in place. No tiles were broken. And Verl said, "Look at how nice it works." He turned on the faucet and I admired his handi-work. Paul admired it when he came to work on Monday. A neighbor tried it and remarked that it flowed and handled beautifully.

And I have mentioned it with pleasure at least once a day for the last two weeks. It might have been easier to call a plumber, but my husband's manhood is still intact. Gosh, I hope nothing else breaks.

Chapter 15
Go Ahead, Laugh

Go ahead and laugh. It is good for you. I have been reading accounts of research done by a group at Harvard. They have studied two groups of men, over their adult life spans, late teens to old age. One group was a class of Harvard students; the other was a group of inner-city Boston youths. They have attempted to answer questions about why it is that some people, even people born into miserable circumstances, are mentally and physically healthy, and others, in spite of every advantage, lead lives of despair.

When I was teaching, I have used the earlier work reported by these researchers in my classes and am always interested in their latest findings. The latest work confirmed conclusions of the earlier studies. People who use mature defenses are able to fare better.

And guess what one of the mature defenses is? Humor.

When I first read this I was very relieved. You see, I have this crazy sense of humor that at times has gotten me into trouble. It is a relief to know that my ability to tolerate the vicissitudes of life by laughing at them and making jokes is healthy.

I always wondered where my peculiar outlook came from. My father, whose parents were born in Ireland, was very witty. His humor was intellectual. I enjoyed it but never had the gift.

My humor, and my brother's, was more crude. When I accidentally dropped the Christmas trimmings from the attic crawl space onto my mother's head as she stood on the bottom step of the ladder, both my brother and I shrieked with laughter. Mom wasn't hurt but she didn't share our hilarity. I was glad to know that another human, my brother, thought the same things were funny.

Years later, Mother had a stroke. Suddenly she was making jokes, just like ours. I think the humor was there all the time behind her dignified school teacher facade.

When Mother had her last stroke she was completely paralyzed, unable to speak or swallow. By her eyes and expression, I knew that she understood. One day, in the hospital, at noon, I leaned over the bed rails and said, "Mom, I'm going down to the lunch room to eat. Now don't you go anywhere until I get back."

My dear mother shook the bed with her laughter. I think that was the last joke we enjoyed together.

When I first became a psychiatric nurse, I worked in a very upscale hospital. The whole place was run on Freudian ideas. In fact it was more Freudian than Freud had been. We nurses were supposed to be blank screens on which the patients could project their internal images. If they asked us a personal question, we were to say, "What need do you have for that information?" Jokes and fun were strictly forbidden. Everything was serious therapy.

I thought the whole thing was silly and demeaned the patients. The setting did offer information I needed, and I tried to comply. But truth will out. Especially when a young woman patient recovered and was discharged. She left me the doll she had carried when she was very disturbed with a note that said, "I thought your children might like to have my doll. Thank Heavens I don't need it any-more. Thanks for everything. I had fun on our walks."

Oops, I was in trouble. My patient knew I had chil-dren and she and I'd had fun. I strove to be careful and hide my humor.

It crept out in graduate school. I expected the worst. Instead my teachers praised what I had done. "Florence, you relieved the patient's anxiety and put the situation into perspective. That was a very creative intervention." Oh, I thought, is that what I did? I thought I was just being funny.

Now that I am married to a farmer, I have absolute permission to exercise my funny bone. My husband has a similar sense of humor. He also likes practical jokes but I told him the first year of our marriage to "..knock it off. I get mad." (I told my nursing school roommates the same. They never did put my mattress on the fire escape or put body parts left over from the OR in my bed.)

The every day farm disasters, ones where no one is hurt, become after a little while, humorous stories. Gentle jokes work better than nagging around here and create a more pleasant atmosphere.

I was pleased to read this research and learn that because I use humor to make life easier, I will probably live longer. One thing I know without research, laughing makes me happy.

Chapter 16
Shoot-out at Chicken Corral

We don't settle livestock disputes in the West with guns anymore, do we? Well, some people do. Let me tell you about an incident that occurred at my Mother-in-law's small ranch a few miles from here in the Willamette Valley.

Mother, Ruby, is a woman of eighty-eight years who is a loving mother, doting grandmother and independent person. She was raised on a ranch in Idaho and takes care of her little place with occasional help from the family. She has a filbert orchard and raises berries. She no longer has livestock, just a blind dog and a few cats.

A new family moved into a house adjacent to hers and they seemed like nice people. Mother couldn't communicate very well with them because the adults spoke little English and Mother is slightly deaf, but they managed to begin a neighborly relationship.

Then the neighbors began to raise game roosters. Each cock had its own little house and was tethered to it. The hens roamed free. At first it wasn't a problem. When they laid eggs in Mother's bushes, she gathered them up and took them to the owners. They graciously returned the eggs. Mother is an early riser, and doesn't wear her hearing aid at night, so the early morning crowing of the roosters did not bother her.

However as the chicken population increased they became a nuisance. When they dug up the roots of Ruby's favorite rose bushes, she was angry. She told the neighbors that they would have to confine their chickens. They smiled and said, "Yes."

Nothing happened. The hens began roosting on her car. Finally she called the sheriff and asked for help. The sheriff came and spoke with the neighbor and told him that Mother could legally kill the chickens if they got on her place. The neighbor said, "Is O.K. Tell her to kill them."

The hens scratched her tulip bulbs out of the ground. The neighbor did nothing.

Then in true old west style, son-in-law Jim rode to the rescue in his Blazer. Jim is an impressive looking man. He is over six feet and has broad shoulders. The gray sprinkled in his black hair lends dignity. His voice is slightly louder than most and he speaks precisely. Perhaps this is a trait acquired from twenty years in the Army. Colonel Jim is not a man to ignore.

He announced to the neighbor that he was managing the chicken problem for Ruby. "I'll give you a week to get those chickens penned up. If they are not confined in a week, I'll kill them."

Again the neighbor said yes, and did nothing.

A week later Jim rode in, armed with a twenty-two pistol loaded with bird shot.

Bang! Bang! Bang!

The neighbor rushed out. Three chickens lay dead, shot through the head.

The people who live on the other side of the neighbor also rushed to their yard. They began to cheer. They, too, were being scratched out of their landscape.

Bang! Bang!

Two more hens bit the dust.

The neighbor rushed up to Jim. "You crazy, Man? You can't shoot my chickens."

"I told you to pen them up."

"I go to call the Sheriff." The man ran to his house.

The Marion County Sheriff's Department responds quickly and in a few minutes the same deputy who had been there earlier arrived. By then five more chickens had been executed. Jim gathered up the corpses and dumped them over the neighbor's ineffective fence onto his property.

The people from the other side of the neighbors arrived. They volunteered to testify for Jim if it should be needed.

The Deputy inspected Jim's gun and ammunition and questioned him about the direction he had aimed.

Then he turned to the irate neighbor and told him to pen up his chickens before they were all dead.

Jim holstered his pistol and rode off in his Blazer. Ruby's ranch was safe from marauding poultry.

That night the neighbor and all his relatives gathered up the last of his hens and put them in boxes and makeshift cages,and even inside their cars. In a few days, a high wire fence enclosed the neighbor's yard, and the remaining chickens are now happily scratching and picking in their own back yard.

The West is still a little wild. Cowboys just ride Blazers or pick-ups these days.

Chapter 17
Remembering D-Day

Four years ago near the fiftieth anniversary of D-Day I read all the papers and watched the televised accounts of that momentous day, and I was unaccountably depressed and tearful. I knew all the facts about the campaign. I was seventeen when it happened. I had just graduated from high school and had signed up for the U. S. Cadet Nurse Corps. My brother, John, two years my senior, had been in England, and we knew that he would be in the invasion.

Somehow, then, the invincibility of youth and the needs of the times took over. I worried about what Johnny was experiencing but I was sure he would come home. After all he was the kid that swam across the Beaver River when he was nine — on Good Friday, had been in the CCCs and earned extra money by jumping out of planes at the airport. He also was a trick motorcycle rider. He was good at risky activities.

But images of my parents' worried faces appeared in my thoughts. Now that I had been a mother and a nurse, I knew how fragile and how precious life is. I suspect that my feelings and my tears were in part the anguish that I repressed fifty years ago, and also the new insights that age brings.

I called Johnny, something I did frequently. He lived three thousand miles away, but we had always been close, and we grew even closer as we aged.

After we talked about the family news, I talked about the D-Day anniversary. Johnny never talked much about it. Perhaps because he so often was dealing with a later war. After W.W.II he learned how to fly and enlisted in the Air Force Reserves—and was called back for Korea. He stayed for an another enlistment period and picked up his second discharge. His business—he was a mechanic—suffered a setback, and in order to support his family he tried to rejoin. He was too old for the Air Force, but the Army was glad to have him back—and he went to Viet Nam.

Once, newly back from W.W.II and not yet twenty one, he sat in the back seat of a car with me. It was after a double date. John had been drinking. He told me about the fighting in France and the fear, horror and adrenaline rush. He cried and I comforted him. He has brushed off my questions ever since.

During our phone call, I tried again. "You were in the combat engineers, and landed on Omaha Beach, right?"

"Yeah."

"What wave were you in?"

"The first. We had to get the mines out. But Sis, we had it a lot easier than the guys that came later. We were so well trained. I had four months of Ranger training in England, and the British Commandos trained us too."

"You told me once about a mortar hitting close and blowing your uniform off."

"Yeah, Sis, but that happened later. Let me tell you how I celebrated today. I had some money put aside. I got a bunch of five dollar bills and went down to the V. A. Hospital. I passed the bills out to the guys who are there that have no families. When I was in there I saw how it was for them. My boys and your Shevawn visited. It's bad for the guys who have no one. They were happy to have a little spending money and I enjoyed the day. Now when am I going to see you?"

We made plans to meet that summer at our home community in Pennsylvania, when I would be at my fiftieth high school class reunion. I could hear John's granddaughters laughing and talking in the background. His son and the girls lived with John. He talked a little about his work as a gunsmith and told me about the antique plane he was restoring. He was a licensed airplane mechanic and aerobatics pilot and his retirement was a busy happy time.

Then he said good-by telling me, as always, that he loved me.

When I hung up I decided that John has healed any psychic wounds the wars have given him. I'm sure he has scars, but he refuses to probe them. I determined not to allow nostalgia to diminish the joy I found in life. After all, isn't the freedom to enjoy our blessings what our men fought for?

*Note: John died two years after D Day. I was with him at the veterans hospital when he stopped breathing.

Chapter 18
The Cat Came Down

Nursery people are a diverse group. Some, like my husband, have known since childhood what they wanted to do with their lives. All their efforts were spent with one goal in mind—owning their own nursery and growing beautiful plants. Others have entered the business after a time in other occupations; business, teaching, and the military are often their first professions. Also there are the farmers who weary of the vicissitudes of raising strawberries or wheat and see ornamentals as a more stable crop.

Dick and Sally are close friends. Dick worked in the aerospace industry during the heyday of that field, and longed to grow beautiful trees, rare and lovely conifers. About twenty-five years ago he married Sally and together they worked to realize that dream. Both had been married previously and had children. They bought a farm in Oregon and moved there with her two children. In due time these propagators produced their child, Margie.

Dick has English heritage. He would look at home on a horse, in a red coat, ready to ride with his hounds. He has an aristocratic profile, and his fair skin is usually pink from long hours outside. Sally was raised in Hollywood and is Jewish. She studied botany in College and worked in medical laboratories. She is a pleasant looking woman, with a smiling face.

She and Dick have a passion for waterfowl and when you drive into the driveway of their home and nursery you are met by their flock of geese who honk a greeting. Then you drive past Dick's airplane and then are struck by Sally's flower garden. Prize roses stretch along the drive with beautiful blue shrubs behind. Next you hear the dogs barking—Sally raises Fox Terriers—and as you enter the house, assorted cats meow greetings. The house is filled with flowers, rare orchids, wild flowers and flowers from Sally's garden. They bloom amid the antiques and art. If you chance to go to the bathroom, you will be greeted by Mother, the biggest gold fish I've ever seen, swimming alone in her tank on the counter. An oil painting of an otter hangs over the bathtub and the pictures on the other walls invite you to tarry. Down the hall in the study, Dick has his collection of Indian arrowheads, a collection worthy of a museum. Maria, a Mexican-American teenager, may be running the sweeper, before she dashes off to the English class that Sally arranged for her. You open the baby gate into the kitchen and Sally herds one of the puppies into the back hall. Then she invites you to sit at the antique flower filled table, while she brews you a cup or tea.

I love Sally's parties. She collects interesting people with even more passion than she spends collecting antiques, waterfowl, or flowers. Several years ago, I volunteered to finish a needle point project that Sally's daughter had begun. It turned out to be a job that took months of evening hours, before the television. Sally wanted to repay me, and I demanded a price. I wanted to be invited to all of her large parties. She agreed, and I am the happiest guest there because I know what a good time I am going to have.

Sally had a little female cat named Blackie. Sally had taken her to the vet, with whom she has a close relationship—no wonder, with so many pets. Blackie had had surgery to remove the ability to reproduce. The animal was upset by the surgery and by the results of the instructions from the vet, "Keep her inside for a week." This meant she had to use the litter box and couldn't cavort with the half dozen cats that frolicked on the front porch.

The day after Blackie came home from her surgery, someone allowed her to slip out the door. Sally searched frantically for her adolescent pet but Blackie eluded her. Late that night, Margie came home from college and as she passed through the yard, she heard a faint meow from far up in an old cherry tree. She came in and told Sally and together they went out with their strongest flashlight. They flashed the light and there in the top of the tree clung a frightened little cat, Blackie.

Dick is an early riser and had long since retired. The women tried calling, coaxing and a lure of anchovies. Blackie clung to her perch and resisted all entreaties to come down. Sally and Margie were forced to go to bed and leave her there. All night long the mournful wail of this stranded convalescent filled the women's ears and dreams. Toward morning, Blackie dozed off and all three slept fitfully.

Dick, unaware of the crisis, rose early, fixed his own breakfast and left the nursery with a truckload of nursery stock. By the time Sally and Margie got up, Blackie was again crying for rescue.

Margie tried to climb the tree, while Sally stood, wrung her hands and called, "Be careful." The climber was able to get near the cat, but the animal was just beyond her reach and the branches between them were too small to bear her weight. Margie returned to earth and Blackie wailed even louder.

Sally went into the house and called the local volunteer fire department.

"Sorry, Ma'm," was the answer, "we don't go out to rescue cats. She'll come down when she is hungry enough."

Sally's pleas about her pet's recent surgery did not shake the fireman.

The electric company wasn't even polite when Sally called them.

She and Margie inspected the ladders Dick kept in the barn. None was long or strong enough to reach poor Blackie.

About ten Dick returned from his delivery to find his wife and daughter standing beneath the old cherry tree pleading with meowing Blackie.

"What's going on?"

They told him.

He disappeared into the tool shed and returned with the chain saw. Before they could protest, he applied the saw to the tree trunk, stopping just before he had sawed through. He gave the old tree a final push and it toppled slowly toward the ground, the branches breaking the impact of the trunk's descent.

Blackie rode the tree as it fell and then leaped gracefully to the ground. She ran through the open door into the house and dashed under a bed.

Dick remarked, "That old tree wasn't good anymore. I'll cut it up for firewood when I have time." He headed toward the tool shed to put the chain saw away.

Margie hurried into the house to make sure Blackie was all right. Sally remained in the yard looking at the felled tree, a favorite antique, and wondering what sort of a tree she should plant to replace it.

Chapter 19
Varmints

Oregon is the Wild West. Right? Well, anyway it is the West. Somehow when I lived *back East* I imagined that anywhere west of Kansas was inhabited by wild animals. I remember how concerned my mother was when I planned a vacation in the Rockies. She was afraid that I would be bitten by a snake or mauled by a bear.

Well, we do have a few wild critters here. Most are up in the mountains. Recently on Mt Hood a cougar followed some hikers for four miles and scared the wits out of them. The rangers figured the cat was just curious, but to avoid trouble they closed the trail to hikers.

A black bear who was living in a cow pasture was shot because the authorities were afraid that it might get in a fight with some home owner over a garbage can. A young cougar was found treed by a dog in a suburban area. It was feeding lavishly on the rabbits who lived on a nearby golf course. It was tranquilized by a dart and trucked away to the mountains. One of two bachelor elks who took up residence in a park near downtown Portland wasn't so lucky. He died as the result of the tranquilizer.

What wild creatures live here on the nursery? We do have a few deer who leave their tracks in the fields. They also pick out two or three arbor-vitae and use them to sharpen their horns. Deer tracks lead to trees with broken branches and scarred bark. Since they use the same trees, we consider the damage an acceptable loss—our contribution to the local wildlife.

Verl has seen a coyote a few times and we hear foxes barking in the woods. Half tame opossums eat the cat food while wary felines keep a safe distance. These critters are so omnivorous that they try to eat the dishes and have taken a bite out of one.

Skunks let us know they are here by their scent. A mother skunk and her baby invaded the head propagation house driving out our employees. They in turn turned a hose on this black and white lady and vanquished her. When she scooted into the tall grass, we saw that her foot was stuck in a tomato juice can. The women and I, all mothers, were worried. How would she survive and raise her babies? Late that evening, Verl and I were walking down by our pond and Mrs. Skunk and two babies came out of the weeds. She was limping but the can was gone. The wild family scurried into the grass and we carefully retreated up the lane.

A friendly gopher snake has lived in the greenhouse for years. The sky is frequently filled with the gliding circles of red tailed hawks. And our bold and sassy blue jays steal the cat's food.

But none of these creatures is found only in the West. There are more deer in Pennsylvania. When I lived there I had fresh venison to replenish the supply in the freezer every year, as did all my neighbors. Sunday dinner in the Fall was often a feast of pheasant.

However in the Willamette Valley we do have the biggest and most prolific gophers that I have ever seen. They happily burrow all through the fields, digging tunnels through rootballs, and making trees difficult to dig. Verl uses the gas eradication method that he and my brother perfected but still the toothy little devils multiply. Recently I bought Verl a statue of a happy gopher. The fellow is holding a shovel and his pockets are full of potatoes. Verl loved his gift and put it just outside the office door. I suspect that he has a certain grudging respect for these little fellows who dig as well as he does.

When I first moved to Oregon, I went outside one morning and there on the sidewalk was a creature I had never before seen. It was five inches long, greenish brown with spots and had horns on its head. No legs. Ugh, what was that? My neighbor enlightened me. I was looking at a slug. They inhabit the Willamette valley and happily suck the juice from all the green plants they can find. As they crawl along they leave a trail of slime, a sort of sluggy calling card. For a change of diet, they crawl into the cat's dish and try a little dried cat food. Then they crawl out and have my rhododendron for dessert. Verl says they lay a million eggs each year. When he sees one he stamps it with his boot. I stay back because I don't like to be splashed by slug juice, even though it is digested chlorophyll.

Methods for eradication of these critters abound. (Oregonians, forgive me. I know you've heard it all but I hope my book has a wide audience.) One method is to fill a pie pan with beer and embed it in the ground. The slugs crawl to it and either drink themselves to death or drown. A gruesome method is to sprinkle salt on the poor fellows. The principal of osmosis operates and all their body juices leak out to dilute the salt. That seems even more cruel than Verl's quick stamp. Slug bait sells well in Oregon stores.

Oregonians have a certain fondness for slugs. You can buy slug tee shirts and figurines in the stores. Recently an attractive Oregon woman was named Slug Queen and will reign over the Slug Festival to be held in Eugene. There will be a parade and events such as the Secretary's Type-

writer Toss and a bed race. Queen Zinnia will open the fes-
tivities wearing a green and gold gown—" wonderful iri-
descent slimy stuff."

Since I've lived in Oregon for more than twenty
years, I've joined the rest of the citizens and have developed a certain grudging affection for these little slime balls.

My enemy varmints are moles. They feast on bulbs.
I have planted scores of crocus and tulips and after one
year, they are gone and in their place is a mound of fine
Willamette Valley soil. The cats use it as a convenient litter
box. Anyone who drives by the yard takes one look and
says "Umm, moles."

A few years ago, one sunny April Sunday, Verl and I
drove several miles to enjoy the fields of a tulip grower.
Acres and acres of gorgeous tulips stretched toward the
blue mountains in the distance. Verl loves flowers and
plants even more than I do. He ran from row to row, trying
to choose what he would buy and then gave up and bought
two hundred.

"Won't the moles get them?"

"No, I know how to fix them so they can't," said my
clever nurseryman husband.

He dug a trench around our brick patio and lined it
with chicken wire, the fine mesh type. Then he put the dirt
back in the trench and planted dwarf box wood and a hundred tulip bulbs. We packed up the rest and sent them to
my daughters. The next Spring they were wonderful. Every time I looked out the kitchen or living room windows,
my heart lifted. We had defeated the moles.

For that year! Then the fat little fellows got smart.
They came out of the ground—when the cats weren't
around—and walked across the top of the chicken wire
barrier. Then they burrowed back into the earth and feasted

on tulip bulbs. One spot seemed safe. There was a wide cement walk separating the bed from the lawn. I had tulips there a year longer. Then a big mound of dirt appeared on each side of the walk and my tulips disappeared.

The next spring I returned to the tulip farm and asked, "What do you do about moles?"

"Plant gladiolas," said the expert.

At the fair this year there was a display sponsored by a chemical company. The corpses of gophers, moles and various kinds of mice were displayed. I assume they were stuffed because the fair lasted twelve days. I had a close view of the body of one of my enemies. I couldn't help but admire its soft gray coat, and its snout and funny little feet were—well, cute. The salesman admitted to me that the poison he was selling would also poison cats, "But they wouldn't get it." I thought of my thirteen (plus or minus) hopeful felines, who spend days crouched at the opening of the moles tunnels.

"No thanks," I said when I was offered a sample. Since I can't beat the moles, maybe I'll just make pets of them.

Chapter 20
It's Hard to Keep a Good Man Down

Sometime in the middle of the night my bed partner told me that his knee hurt. But when six o'clock came he was up and out to begin the day's work in the nursery. About nine o'clock he came limping in, moaning. His knee was hot, swollen, and exquisitely painful.

Gout, we concluded. He had always gotten it in his big toe, but it can affect any joint. He took his medicines for gout, informing me that one of them was derived from the autumn crocus. Then we waited for the relief that usually occurs half an hour after the drugs.

Relief didn't come. Instead he had a chill and then a fever. Oh, oh, an infection! I called our HMO and then drove him to the urgent care clinic. The doctor confirmed my diagnosis, prescribed an injection of an antibiotic and more to follow by mouth. He aspirated the knee and took a culture. Then he gave strict orders that Verl should not bear weight on the knee, but use crutches. He also prescribed hot packs.

Paul, Verl's son and right hand man at the nursery, had taken four month old Danny to the doctor and wasn't at the nursery when we returned. I drove up as close to the door as possible and let my wounded spouse out.

Imagine my horror when this feverish man, hopped over a hedge, mounted his three wheeler and tore off to instruct the workers. Then his mother arrived, so I held my tongue when he came clumping into the house.

I settled him in his recliner, elevated his leg, applied hot wet packs to the knee and tucked a blanket around him. Then I served his lunch, lots of fluids, brought the medication and offered great gobs of sympathy.

I also moved the phone close and tried to get his two way radio going. Then every few minutes I ran notes out to Javier and Ernesto. "Pack up 200 kinnikinnick and get it ready for UPS", "Plant the upright maples in one row and the spreading ones in the next so they are shaded." Etc. and etc.

Then "Dear, run out to the loading dock and see if those fifteen Baby Blue Eyes are ready for the truck."

My, I was busy. By evening his knee didn't hurt and his temperature was down to 100.

The next day he disappeared from the bed at six, as usual. "It won't hurt him to get his own breakfast" I thought and went back to sleep.

When I got up he was lying on the couch, with his leg elevated, reading the paper. He still had a slight fever. He clumped past me and said, "I'm going to sit in my chair."

Then he disappeared. His crutches were in the house, but he wasn't in the house or office. The three wheeler was outside the office door.

I was mad. It seemed that he would only yield to sickness if he were in severe pain. I had fantasies about taking off and letting him fend for himself. Maybe I'd go to that Meryl Streep movie. Verl wouldn't take me because he is boycotting Meryl Streep because of her role in the alar scare.

About eleven he came limping in, drawn and bent. I yelled at him, as any good nurse/wife would. Then I settled him in his chair, applied the hot packs, brought the fluids and began to run errands.

He sees the doctor at eight thirty tomorrow. That time interferes with a meeting of a committee I should attend. Part of me says that if he can drive around the nursery, he can take himself to the doctor. The other part says, maybe I should go with him so I can hear the doctor's instructions.

It sure is hard to keep a good man down.

Chapter 21
What's In A Name?

I am sitting at my desk admiring the beauty of Mrs.G W. Leak. I don't know who the original Mrs. Leak was, but someone named a lovely rhododendron for her. Every Spring I pick a few clusters of the pink petaled, magenta throated blossoms and bring them into the house to brighten gray days.

I am amused by botanical names. Yes, I know they are long, difficult to pronounce and impossible (for me) to spell. But they do keep the world of horticulture in order. Imagine what confusion would exist if every language had only its own common name for each plant. It would be easier if the botanical names were in English, rather than in Latin, but then our friends, the French, would be sure to object.

I did study Latin in high school and that has made learning the botanical names less difficult. I found it helpful when I studied nursing, and it improved my vocabulary in English. I am sorry that most schools no longer offer Latin. However, I think that Spanish, which I am studying now, would offer similar advantages with the added plus of being a living language.

The botanical names tell the genus and species of the plant. Then, if the plant is a certain variety, that is added also. Someone who developed that beautiful rhododendron wanted to honor a lady named Mrs. G. W. Leak, and named the variety for her.

One of the plants my husband grows is Picea Pungens Glauca, 'Hoopsi'. It is a blue spruce with grayish blue foliage. It was a chance seedling that was discovered in the 1940's in the Hoops nursery in Boskoop, Holland. All of our trees of this variety are propagated by grafting and are clones of the original tree. My husband and I have visited Boskoop. Seeing the trees in the original nursery was a little like seeing the ancestors of your children. We were excited.

Many varieties that are named for people have had an i or two added to the end of the variety name. Two examples are: Ilex Cornuta Burfordii (Burford Holly) and Camaecyparis Lawsoniana Elwoodii (Ellwood Cypress).

Thirty years ago my husband noticed, among a bed of hundreds, a blue spruce seedling that had unusual properties. He sat it aside for several years, watched and then began to propagate from it. It is slow growing, very dense and establishes terminal dominance even without staking. This means that a piece of wood taken from a branch and grafted onto a common blue spruce understock begins immediately to act as though it were the top of the tree. It has nice turquoise color and each tree is exactly like the others. After he had several thousand trees, he applied for and was rewarded a patent.

He named the tree 'Baby Blue Eyes'. Instead of two i's he used Eyes. It is also named for his first wife, Alice Knox Holden, who was a blue eyed blond. It was his special name for her. Alice died when she was forty-two, and all those beautiful little trees are a memorial to her.

The Iseli nursery in Boring also has a special blue spruce variety. They weren't so romantic as Verl. Their very bushy blue spruce variety is called Fat Albert. I don't know who Albert is, but I hope he is happy.

I have told Verl that the next plant he develops should be named for him, 'Holdenii'. Then the one after that I want to be mine, 'Hardestyi', or 'Flossyi' (So now you know, Flossy is my nickname). Since the chances of a small nursery like ours, patenting three new plants are small, I am afraid we won't be immortalized by living, growing plants. Gosh, what if the plant was a crab apple tree or a thorny bush. Would I want that named for me?

The next time I go to the library, I must use the plant encyclopedia and look up Mrs. G. W. Leak. I'd like to know who that lady was.

Chapter 22
A Coon Tale

Remember the old saying, "You can take the boy away from the farm but you can't take the farm out of the boy." That certainly seems true of Verl, although it is other people who persist in calling forth the farmer in him. The worst offenders are my daughters and sons-in-law. The phone calls begin before our visits, and we arrive at the airports, loaded with baggage such as nematodes—microscopic worms destined to eat the grubs in Susan's lawn— or a sprayer for Shevawn and George. Tasks like pruning and planting trees always need to be done when Verl visits.

On the way from the airport to Shevawn and George's home in Hingham, a suburb south of Boston, the following conversation took place.

George said, "Verl, some animal is climbing up on the kitchen roof, and dumping right next to the skylight. We can't open the skylight anymore because it smells awful. What could that be?"

"It's not your cats, is it?" They have two felines, who were pampered, until the children arrived.

"No. They use Shevawn's flower beds."

"Well maybe it's a coon."

"There're lots of them around."

The subject was dropped when Shevawn interjected that Johnny, who is two, has almost trained himself. The grandchildren are more interesting to me than Hingham's wildlife.

The visit proceeded, with trips to the aquarium, lobster dinners, and hours of just admiring our three little grandsons. Grandpa and George built a sandbox and horticultural advice was freely given.

Shevawn and George live in a house that was built in 1740. Connected to the house, which was a dairy house, is a barn (the largest walk-in closet in the world) a silo that contains an apartment, and an ancient sheep shed. The city won't permit the removal of the sheep shed, which is an eyesore, because of its historic value. George obligingly allows his neighbors to store their boats in it.

One night at dinner, George mentioned the mystery of the hot water tank. This tank is in the barn and supplies hot water to the tenant who lives in the silo. When it stopped working, George called the repairman who discovered that someone had turned off the switch that controls the pilot light. Embarrassed that he hadn't discovered that before he called for help, George turned on the switch which is in an enclosed area under the tank. But it continued to go off. Verl promised to investigate.

The hot water tank is in an enclosed room in the barn. The door was closed and locked and the only other opening to the room was a six inch wide hole in the concrete under the tank where air entered. The men squatted down close and studied the mechanism. Who and why would anyone shut off the heat?

Suddenly they heard a hissing growl. They rose and stood back. There was a scurrying sound and then they glimpsed a fluffy ringed tail just as it disappeared down the opening under the tank.

The culprit was a coon. He had found a nice warm place to nest, and when it got too warm, he turned off the switch.

Now the question was, How do we get rid of the coon?

Verl had a ready answer. He and George would trap the animal in a *Have a Heart Trap*. This is the brand name of an animal trap that entices the prey into a small cage to eat a delicious morsel, the bait. As soon as the bait is disturbed, a door is sprung and the animal cannot leave. We had used one of these traps to catch our seven wild kittens when we wanted to take them to be neutered. Shevawn, a wildlife lover, would consent to this only when we assured her that the animal would not be hurt.

Finding a trap in Hingham was not a problem. There are lots of woods around the town and evidently lots of wildlife. We found the trap in a hardware store and I bought it for George as a birthday gift.

That evening the trap was baited with nice smelly sardines. The barn was secured so that no children could wander in and the mighty hunters watched television with their ears cocked to hear the trap spring.

They heard the twang and rushed from the living room through the door into the barn.

The trap was closed tight and the bait was gone, but no raccoon was present.

The next evening we went to the shore for a lobster dinner. Two lobsters were too much for me, and we brought a doggy bag home. The men gleefully baited the trap with a lobster body.

The next morning they rushed out to find a nice fat coon sleeping in the trap. Now what were they to do?

They called the Humane Society, Animal Control, and the Nature Conservancy, and received the same answer. There are too many coons. We have stopped taking them.

George had no gun. If the trap were opened the coon would come out fighting and it could be dangerous. They do sometimes carry rabies.

George suggested that they drown it. If they dropped the cage in a fifty gallon barrel.... But they couldn't find a barrel that big.

Could they gas it? They put the trap back in the box it had come in and cut a small round hole. They inserted the exhaust of the car in the hole and started the vehicle. There was some coughing and scrambling in the box and then silence. Well, they thought, the deed is done.

But they wanted to hide the evidence. The boys' favorite video is Bambi, and all the animals in their story books have human qualities. Besides that, Shevawn is very soft hearted. It seemed best to avoid explanations. They put a shovel in the car and loaded the box, cage and coon into the trunk. They would bury him in the woods.

Driving through town, seven miles from the house, the men spotted a dumpster. No one was around to see. They decided to leave the body in it.

They stopped the car and unloaded the box. When they opened it they looked into the bright eyes of a very live coon. He chattered and scolded the humans who trapped him.

There was a chain link fence by the dumpster and woods beyond. The men gave up their goal of extermination. George held the trap and Verl maneuvered the door with the shovel. As soon as it opened, Mr. Coon jumped out, and chattering over his shoulder in coon language, hurried off to the woods.

George called the police station to find out how one gets a permit for a gun. In Massachusetts you must have a permit to own any kind of a gun. My brother, who is a gunsmith, visited from upstate New York, and promised to see that George got a suitable weapon, as soon as he had a permit. We flew home to Oregon.

Two days after we arrived home, Verl received a call from George. The coon is back. The bait has been gone every morning, even when it was wired to the platform, but the trap hasn't been sprung. A fresh pile of feces has been deposited on the kitchen roof. Shevawn is feeling even more distress at the idea that such an intelligent and persistent creature must be killed.

The tenant may be taking cold showers this summer while George battles the wily raccoon. Maybe if he puts a screen over the hole.......

Chapter 23
Ila

I have been accused of being a Pollyanna or an incurable optimist. During the years I worked in psychiatric settings the term denial was sometimes attached to me by my fellow workers.

I plead guilty. I do approach bad situations with the hope of making them better or at least bearable. And I hope that perhaps there might be opportunities for something good to evolve from them.

A high school classmate, Ila Fields, had a lot to do with the way I approach life. I didn't know her well when we were in school. The class of the rural Pennsylvania school was small but Ila and I were from different parts of the district.

In 1944 when we graduated, I joined the Cadet Nurse Corps and went to nursing school in Philadelphia. By the time I finished, the war was over and I returned home to marry my sweetheart who had just returned from the Navy. We moved into a small house and I began working as a nurse at the local hospital. The late forties was a time of high spirits and boundless optimism. We had been children during the depression and teenagers during the War. We had survived both times and as young adults we were sure our future was golden.

I learned that my classmate, Ila, had also married a returning serviceman. She and her husband were building a house in the corner of a lovely meadow.

Word came to the hospital where I worked that we would be getting a new patient, one with bulbar polio. We readied an isolation room and ordered the iron lung be brought from the supply room. I was assigned to be the patient's private nurse.

It was Ila. She was very ill with a high fever and rapidly ascending paralysis. We placed her in the huge metal cylinder, reaching through the tight rubber cuffs to position her, insert a catheter and try to make her comfortable. Her head was thrust through a rubber cuff and rested on a small shelf outside. Since her breathing was impaired the lung breathed for her, changing pressure so that her lungs expanded to take in air and contracted to expel it. Ila could speak only during the time air was being forced out of her lungs.

Every day for the next week, gowned and masked, I was with Ila. Caring for her physical needs was strenuous, but nothing was so difficult as listening to this young woman, whose life until then had been so much like mine. The words came in a rush as the bellows underneath the iron lung whooshed and forced air from her lungs.

"Oh, Flossie, I don't want to die.....I love Chuck so much....I'm pregnant.....We are building our house......Please God, don't let me die!"

I reached through the cuffs to hold her hand and let my tears collect in my mask. When I left the room to get supplies, I would see Chuck, Ila's tall husband, crying in his mother's arms.

At the end of the week, Ila ceased raging against her fate, slipped into a coma, and died.

For years after when I passed the meadow and saw the abandoned foundation of Chuck and Ila's house, I cried.

My life moved on, and as happens to everyone, I've had my share of disappointments. My husband found another love and our marriage ended. Aching from betrayal and loneliness, I took on the task of raising my little girls alone. Divorce was rare then and many considered a divorcee a fallen woman. Dating, after the security of marriage, was fraught with ups and downs. My career has been successful, but as in all working situations, there were difficult times.

In those moments when I have been tempted to feel sorry for myself, I think of Ila. Now I have had fifty more years of living than she had. I have wonderful children and grandchildren. My career has given me great satisfaction. I've traveled and had adventures. Nearly twenty years ago I married a special man, the love of my life.

Life is full of everyday pleasures—friends, books, music, satisfying work. I am determined to not be distracted by the irritating trivia of existence—things like taxes, petty quarrels, or the infirmities of age—but to enjoy all I can of this wonderful gift, life. When my determination slips, I remember Ila, and give thanks for the lesson she gave me.

Chapter 24
Ladies, Seize the Power

I t is my considered scientific opinion that testosterone predisposes males to grasp the television remote control firmly in their strong hands and never let it go.

Even my nice husband insists that he be in charge of the television remote control. (He also always drives when we are together, even in my car.) Now he isn't as bad as my son-in-law, George, the champion channel surfer. George watches three movies at one time, a practice that drives me mad.

Verl loves to watch football on the big screen television that I bought him for his birthday about five years ago. We sit in our bedroom in the evenings, each in our recliners with a table loaded with books and magazines between us. The table is a mess. I am always going to organize it, but I never do. The room is our cozy nest.

I have no interest in football and much prefer to read. I could sit in the living room but with its wall of glass it seems cold at night. Besides, I enjoy being in the same room as my husband. So I sit in my chair, try to block out the sound of the television, and read.

However I do get annoyed when I hear my spouse snore. If I tip toe over to remove the remote from his grasp, he wakes with a start, and turns it louder—to keep himself awake.

Sometimes I am watching a favorite program and suddenly my hero and heroine are replaced by a foot ball game. "What did you do?" I cry.

"I'm just checking the score."

Then one wonderful day I was in the store and saw a display of remotes. They weren't very expensive. I asked a passing clerk, "Will these work with any TV?"

"Yes, " she replied, "just follow the directions to program it."

I bought one for twelve dollars, and brought it home. I programmed it and placed it by my chair.

That night when football was on television, and my husband went to sleep, I pressed "mute" and had a half hour of blissful silence. When I heard him stir, I turned on the sound and he woke up and said, "What's the score?"

My delight over my new found toy was too good to keep, so I told him that I too, had the power.

Now if he tries to pull a sneaky switch, I can switch it back. He's stopped doing it. I can control the volume without having to justify it. Never has anyone gained such a feeling of power for a measly twelve dollars.

When I was doing marital counseling, I found that there was more conflict between couples over money than any other issue. I would try to help the man and woman work out an agreement about who paid what bills, what expenses each was free to make on his/her own and what things required consultation and mutual agreement. Very often part of the solution would be separate checking accounts.

No one ever consulted me about struggles over who controls the television set. But if someone ever did, I have a new solution to the problem. "Buy your own remote. It only costs twelve dollars."

Chapter 25
The Best News

Every Wednesday evening I walk to the mail box to retrieve our copy of the *Silverton Appeal Tribune and Mt. Angel News*, the weekly local paper. Since we don't live in either town, and our children are grown, we aren't much interested in the reports of the political events of the towns or the high school sports. But there is one section that I look forward to reading with pleasure. It is called Public Safety and contains news of police and fire activities.

This week only two items were listed under Fire. I guess the wet weather has solved the grass and brush fire problems that filled this section last fall. The police list items by date and time, and in terse Joe Friday language, state the facts—just the facts.

Behind the facts there is pathos, human tragedy, and humor. The dry reporting highlights the unstated emotions.

My, the police are busy around here! Portlanders may have trouble getting the police to respond to car thefts and burglaries, but the Mt. Angel and Silverton men in blue will help with any emergency.

I am amused by the news listed under a heading, Suspicious Circumstances. They tell you a lot about small town life. Two items, at separate addresses, read something like: Caller reported two men crawling through window of a nearby home. Officer investigated and determined that they lived there.

I guess that will teach those people to carry an extra set of keys.

Strange vehicles that contain suspicious looking men are also reported. They are never there when the police arrive. One was seen every morning and as it drove off, the observer noticed a man, scrunched down in the seat. It isn't wise to stay all night at your girlfriend's house in a small town.

Two men were reported to be standing on a street corner carrying a large white bag. The officer who investigated reported that it was full of laundry.

The animal complaints are always good for a chuckle. Officer attempted to catch an injured duck. It eluded him. Twice this week someone's pesky mules got out and wandered through the town.

The officers responded when a distraught (my adjective) mother reported that her daughter was suicidal. They took her to the hospital. A counselor reported that a client was extremely agitated. The police also took him to the hospital.

A caller reported that someone was removing the tires from his vehicle. It turned out that they were being repossessed. The officer stood by to keep the peace.

Every week there are reports of runaway teenagers. One item added the word *again*. What anguish there must be behind that word. The terse statements about domestic problems mask a world of pain and disappointment.

The police do apprehend criminals and deal with traffic accidents. There are small drug busts. The larger ones are reported in detail in other sections of the paper. There are reports of shoplifting, drunken driving, and burglaries. Occasionally the police pick up a paroled convict and return him to prison.

The metropolitan papers tell of a new idea, community policing. It seems that in small towns the police have always practiced community focused work. I may be amused by the published police report, but I feel much safer because the police are guarding us and all our neighbors.

Chapter 26
Where Do the Truck Drivers Go....?

"Where do the Truck Drivers go between 8 A.M. when they call and say they are in Portland and on their way down for a load, and 5:30 P. M. when they finally arrive — after the workers have gone home?"

Sally posed this weighty question as we sat at the table in her kitchen, drinking tea and admiring the humming bird that hovered outside the window. A motherly basset hound and a feisty adopted kitten rolled around on the floor. Sally's favorite blue jay, the Jewish one, pecked at the bagel on the bird feeder that hung in the old apple tree.

Now before I continue this, I need to say that 98% of the truckers who come to our nurseries are stable professionals. They take pride in delivering their loads and serving their customers. But they don't make very good stories. It is the two percent that supply the tales that nursery people tell at meetings— the *let-me-tell-you-what-happened* stories that come after the speaker is finished and everyone has one more drink.

Back to Sally's question. "Maybe he has a lady somewhere," I suggested.

"That's possible," Sally said. "One of our regular fellows has a lady come here."

It seems that this driver arrives once a year to pick up a load to go to the Mid-West. There is nothing remarkable about him. He is about forty-five, balding with a little paunch, wears jeans, a plaid shirt and suspenders. But each time the truck arrives, it is followed by a late model Cadillac. A slim flashily dressed woman gets out and climbs up into the cab of the truck. As soon as the truck is parked at the loading dock and the initial paperwork is complete, the driver disappears into the truck.

Dick, Sally's husband, is mildly amused by this as he fantasizes about what is happening in the cab, so close to where he is packing in the root balls of the trees he is sending. The Mexican workers, who are all young men, are so bothered by their imaginations that they can hardly work.

Several hours later, just as the loading is finished, the couple emerges from the cab. She gets in her Cadiliac and, giving a little wave to everyone, drives down the driveway and disappears until the next year. The driver completes the paperwork, as cool and as matter-of-fact as you please. The Mexicans examine him carefully, trying to discern if he had just done what they think he has done. Nothing in his appearance betrays him. Then he says good-by or see you next year, gets in the cab and drives away with his load.

I guess he is a fellow who doesn't believe in wasting time needlessly.

Sally decided to send an orchid plant to her cousin in Dayton, Ohio. It was a rare and beautiful plant and this was a very nice gift. She carefully placed it in the box of a truck that was taking a load of Dick's plants to a retail nursery in Cincinnati and sent it on its way. Then she called her cousin. Evidently her cousin does not have much appreciation of plants because she said that Cincinnati was too far to drive to get the orchid. Sally called me and told me that if my daughter who lives in Cincinnati wanted it, she could pick it up at the nursery. Of course Susan was thrilled.

When Susan called the nursery, she was told that no orchid had arrived. When I checked back with Sally she told me this story.

The driver was an elegant Black man, " One of the best looking men I've ever seen, and smart too. I wondered if he were an actor, driving truck until he gets a break." Sally was sure that her gift and Dick's trees were in good hands. In Chicago, a lady joined this handsome driver and accompanied him on his journey. The couple evidently partied their way across Indiana. Not far from the Ohio border, the ominously flashing lights of a pursing police car appeared in his rear view mirror. Common sense deserted him and he decided to try to outrun the police and escape into Ohio.

As he sped down the road he changed lanes often, weaving in and out of the traffic. The plants in the box of the truck shifted and fell with the movement. Finally he gave up and stopped just short of the Ohio border. In seconds he was under arrest. The police asked what was in the refrigerated truck and he told them. They thoughtfully allowed him to call the owner of the retail nursery, who arrived to pick up a mangled load of trees and plants.

Before the driver was taken away by the police, he pressed several hundred dollars in the nursery owner's hand and instructed him to send the lady back to Chicago in a cab. Perhaps the insurance company will compensate Dick for the damaged load. But in the confusion, Sally's beautiful orchid was lost forever.

I do wish I knew the rest of this story. But like so many stories that we find in real life, it isn't all there. We'll just have to imagine what motivated him.

Most women who drive big trucks are very competent. They have to be to withstand the harassment they are subjected to. Nurserymen are still a little surprised when the person who wheels a huge truck up to their dock turns out to be a tiny blonde woman. They are also very impressed.

However, one woman who drove truck did her gender no good. She arrived at Dick's one day to deliver a load of plastic pots that had been manufactured in Canada. Now, these loads amount to $10,000 to $15,000 worth of this nursery necessity. The woman wheeled her truck in the drive, down past the green houses and around the bend to the barn where they were to be stored. While Dick and his three employees unloaded and stored the pots away, she wandered up and down the aisles of the greenhouses, and through the yard, admiring the plants and animals.

When the truck was empty and the paperwork finished she asked, "Do I go straight ahead to get out of here?"

"There isn't a road that way, just a lane. You need to back up," Dick said.

"I don't know how to do that," the lady driver confessed.

Dick was tempted to tell her he would do it. Then he considered the value of the truck, the fact that he wasn't covered with insurance. He stifled that helpful impulse.

"Well, you could go down the lane and around the field. We leave about ten feet clearance for our equipment. Go down here for about a quarter of a mile, turn left. When you come to the fence, turn left again. Watch out for that wet spot about a hundred feet after the turn. You can cut over into the field there because it isn't planted yet."

The last part of statement represented a generous gesture. Heavy equipment compacts the soil and makes it less fertile. But he wanted to help a lady.

She took off with the truck. Ten minutes later she came walking back. It seems she had not avoided the wet spot. Her truck was stuck.

Dick took a heavy chain and drove down in his caterpillar tractor. He attached the chain and pulled with all the power at his disposal. The truck shuddered but did not move. He tramped back and gathered up three chains, his remaining three tractors and three employees. They all hooked up to the truck and pulled and pulled.

It shuddered, spun and came free of the mud. The driver waved a graceful hand from the window and drove down the lane, into the drive, out on the road and away to Canada.

The workers made a few sexist remarks in Spanish. Dick refrained but he was sure that one attractive Canadian woman would soon learn to back up her semi or quit driving truck

Chapter 27
A Christmas Memory

T he other day I was shopping in a downtown Salem department store. When I went into the rest room, as we females do frequently, I saw a middle aged woman wiping up the floor with towels.

"Did you have a little spill?" I thought maybe I could help.

"I spilled something in my purse and I was trying to wash it out." Then I noticed the compact, comb, cards and all the standard content of a woman's purse spread out on the changing table.

I laughed and said, "What a mess! All your cards. I remember how upset I was the time I dropped my purse in the toilet."

"Tell me about it. I need to know that someday I will think this is funny," said the woman as she turned her purse upside down and shook it over the sink.

Her purse was canvas and she had spilled a coke. The water she was washing it out with had leaked on the floor. I took over the chore of wiping up the floor and told her the story.

I was a single mother, living in Cleveland. Susan and Shevawn were five and nine. The three of us had some special adventures together. I took them places like the zoo, the museums, and movies. The girls loved to go, and these were special times for me.

We had a Christmas-time tradition. Every year we would go to Stirling Linders, a large department store. The store occupied seven floors of a building and had a large inside courtyard. At Christmas season they had a huge Christmas tree there—the largest inside Christmas tree I have ever seen. The kids and I loved it. They would talk with Santa Claus. Susan knew he wasn't a person but the combined hopes of millions of parents, hopes that they could make their children happy. She was charitable on this issue and didn't destroy the illusions of her little sister, Shevawn.

We would shop for gifts for special people, my mother, the girls' father, and their Uncle John. I would step around the corner while they bought my gift. Then we would go to Stouffers, a lovely restaurant for dinner. At this stage the girls still ordered cheeseburgers, even in fancy restaurants. It was much harder to take them out for dinner a few years later when they became devotees of lobster.

Susan was a quiet little girl, with dark blue eyes. Like all children she had her moments, but at nine she had no problems acting grown up in an elegant restaurant. Shevawn, at five was a skinny, bruised, wiggling child, with big dark eyes and buck teeth (Straightened a few years later by a wonderful orthodontist.) She noticed and remembered everything, in spite of the fact that she never stopped moving.

We enjoyed our dinner. I'm sure I had the least expensive meal on the menu, but Stouffers had crystal chandeliers and candles on snowy table clothes, and that was more important than food. As usual, Shevawn ate only half her cheeseburger, so we wrapped it in tissues to take home.

Somehow she dropped it and it rolled under the chair of a distinguished looking man. Before I could admonish her to leave it there, Shevawn was out of her chair and standing at the man's elbow. "Please, Mister, can I get my cheeseburger? It fell under your chair."

The man looked startled, but stood, moved his chair and Shevawn retrieved the next day's lunch.

Back at the table, I composed myself and enjoyed my tea. The sugar packets were not filled with granulated sugar, but with powdered sugar. I remarked about this and of course Shevawn had to inspect. While I was counting out money for the check and placing it on the silver tray, my younger daughter managed to spill powdered sugar all over her newly cleaned navy wool skirt.

Off to the ladies room we went. While Shevawn and Susan were working on her skirt, I went into a booth, and goodness knows how, dropped my purse into the toilet.

The purse was a small leather hat box shaped one, expensive, and a gift from my mother. It and the contents could not be thrown into the trash. So the three of us washed and patted dry my driver's and nursing licenses, pictures of the girls, and yes—their father, money, keys, an address book, etc. Needless to say the lipstick, powder and nonessentials were tossed into the trash. We washed out the purse itself, stuffed it with paper towels and the salvaged contents, and left the restaurant.

It had begun to snow and the Christmas lights had halos around them. Down the street a shabby Santa Claus manned the Salvation Army station and rang his bell. The streets were crowded with happy shoppers and in a few minutes our Christmas spirit returned.

When I finished my story, the woman I was helping laughed and thanked me. As I was driving home that day, I wondered why, what must have been a minor disaster at the time, was one of my fondest memories. Perhaps it is because all three of us remember it vividly. We spend every second Christmas together and one of us always mentions the Stirling Linder tree. Then we laugh together about Shevawn's cheeseburger and the awful thing Mom did to her purse. Now Shevawn is a tall sophisticated business executive, and Susan is a nurse with an administrative position at a city health department. Both are beautiful women and devoted mothers. As we talk and remember together, we are again two children and a woman, determined to make our holiday happy. We have always succeeded.

Chapter 28
Chain Saw Landscaping

For the last few days, every spare moment of my husband's busy life has been devoted to what he calls chain saw landscaping. Verl has a major in landscaping to his credit and the year he spent in Japan, courtesy of the Air Force, gave him a keen appreciation of Japanese gardens. He enjoys transforming an uninteresting piece of ground into a fascinating spot.

However, once the garden is planted he turns his attention to his real passion, the nursery. Meanwhile trees and shrubs grow and his favorite plant, bamboo, runs all over the place. When our front yard, a Japanese garden, was planted eighteen years ago, one day before our wedding reception, it brought gushing expressions of appreciation from all who saw it. Lately, people have referred to it as a jungle.

Yes, I know I could do it myself—if I devoted full time to the project. Frankly I'd rather write and do my volunteering. And when one has a professional landscaper on site, a rather fussy one, meeting his standards would be difficult. I tried to hire Antonio on Saturdays. Antonio is our employee who has a gardener's soul and a strong back. But he wanted to spend time with his wife and family. In desperation, I resorted to a tried and true tactic. I invited thirty people to come for a Mother's Day celebration.

I awoke on a recent Saturday morning to the roar of the chain saw and the beat of loud Latin music. The massacre had begun. The fox tail spruce that had crowded the rhododendrons was chained down and mutilated, followed shortly after by the dragon eye pine in the Japanese garden. The mother tree of our patented blue spruce, Baby Blue Eyes, even had her lower limbs amputated because they were crowding other specimen plants. The unusual shaped Scotch pine, that shaded the path and bridge that leads to the front door had its lower branches sawed off. My study is so much lighter that Verl will no longer be accurate when he calls it Florence's cave.

The workers who were being led in this charge by Verl, smiled happily and remarked about how beautiful it would all be when it was finished. I went outside frequently to admire and spread lavish praise.

The next few days, when they weren't loading truck, digging trees, or weeding in the greenhouses, the guys grubbed out bamboo. Verl arrived and was dismayed to see that a rare dwarf specimen was gone. Hearing this, I rushed out to defend the workers. Who but a bamboo expert would know that was a rare plant? When I got there, I saw that his eyes were twinkling. He assured everyone that it would grow back—what bamboo doesn't?

I had told the children of the families I invited to bring their bathing suits. When I delivered this news to Verl, he groaned. Our pool is in a greenhouse. For a number of reasons, it was never opened last year. It was half full of thick brown gook—dead algae.

On Sunday I went out to see the progress. Verl was in the pool, in his underwear wearing rubber boots. His wet clothes were in a pile by the side of the pool, and he was covered with sweat and smeared with green and brown algae. He was scrubbing the bottom of the pool with a broom. He did look funny but his mood was as foul as the pool. I restrained my impulse to be humorous.

Bless Verl for doing a nasty, dirty job. He is generous and has given me flowers and jewelry. But the gift of his work to clean the pool for me was one of the nicest things I've received.

I don't manipulate people very often and I don't like people who use it as a means to control others. Women historically have resorted to it because we have had so few other options. I always feel a little twinge of guilt when I announce the annual Mother's Day party to my spouse. But not enough to stop me from doing it. It works so well. Year after year, I manipulate my nice husband, and for a few glorious months I am surrounded by a beautiful landscape.

Chapter 29
Dragons and Sprayers

I learn about what is happening at the nursery from bits and pieces of information gleaned here and there. Verl drops a few words at lunch before he turns on the TV to get the news and weather report. I listen to one sided telephone conversations and eavesdrop on conversations in the office between Verl and son Paul. I go out to the propagation house often to practice my Spanish and learn about what is happening from the workers' perspective.

When there is a serious problem or decision to be made, I am involved. Personnel and health problems are my special area and I provide consultation. But my main job is to support and admire the nurseryman—Verl says I am a great admirer.

Once in a long while I am treated — subjected — to a minute by minute description of Verl's day. It usually happens when we go out for dinner shortly after we give our order, and continues until he picks up the check. There isn't space to include a typical story here but I'll hit the high points.

My nice husband begins, "I decided to spray your orchard today. So last night I filled the new sprayer with water and tried it out. It worked perfectly. But this morning — remember I got up at five to spray when the air was still — the darn thing wouldn't start. So I put a little gas in the carburetor and got it going. It worked perfectly and I went down the rows and sprayed out the tank.

"I filled it up again to continue and was going pretty fast when I noticed the ground was wet behind me. The darned plug had come out. I fixed it and filled it up again.

"Then later, I hit a bump. The guys had taken out the last of the nursery stock that was planted in the orchard and hadn't smoothed the ground." Forgive me, expert sprayers, I may not get the rest exactly right. You see, my eyes had glazed over at this point.

"I saw I had a major problem. So I went back to the shop." From here on the story involved nipples, parts that wouldn't fit, screws that had no threads, swearing, cutting, welding, wrenching, a trip to a parts store, and cussing.

I woke up enough to ask, "What's a nipple?"

Finally, of course, my hero got the sprayer fixed and finished the job.

Thinking about this later, it occurred to me that this whole narrative followed the same structure as a novel or the classical folk-tales and myths. The hero starts out determined to reach his goal. He goes along well for a while and then he runs into resistance. Using his skill, strength and cunning he overcomes the resistance and reaches the goal.

No wonder Homer and the other writers of the classics jazzed up their accounts with dragons, sirens, and monsters. If they had told it straight, the ladies who listened might have fallen asleep. Certainly no one would have repeated tales that told how difficult it was to plant vineyards and olive groves on the steep rocky slopes of Greece or what is now Italy. Sailors couldn't tell how lonely and frightened they were, in frail boats, on uncertain seas, with rudimentary navigation. But if they told stories about battling sea monsters, they would be heroes.

At the risk of sounding sexist, I see woman's stories as being different. They are smaller in scope, closer to reality and concern people rather than heroic deeds.

I think we need some good heroic farmer stories. It might counteract the fables that some kids get in school about the selfish farmers harming the environment. Maybe we could enlarge our pests and make monsters out of them—they certainly look monstrous through a microscope. Imagine a giant slug, sucking up all the plants and people. A combine or tractor, given an evil personality, would make a wonderful villain. What about a soil mixing machine that gobbled up people for fertilizer and produced fantastic plants?

There must be some frustrated writers out there who could create wonderful farmer adventure stories. I wouldn't be able to do it. I have enough trouble dealing with and writing about reality. But I promise to buy your book.

Chapter 30
Early Spring

People who don't know the nursery business say things like this to my husband: "You must get to relax a bit in the winter."or, "I guess you get real busy in April with spring planting and all."

My spouse replies, "Yes, but here, Spring starts January first."

Grafting season at our nursery is January and February. Sion wood from a desired nursery plant is grafted onto an ordinary root stock. If done properly, the result is a clone of the desired plant.

During these months if the ground isn't too wet, our "diggers" are in the fields, digging trees. The greenhouse crew still attends to its tasks, and an occasional truck comes in and must be loaded. But the major task is grafting trees.

A group of men sit at a table in the enclosed room near the machine shed. Loud Spanish music blares from the radio and the electric heater makes the room toasty and comfortable. They do the easy grafts: maples, dogwoods, and hazelnuts.

Across the asphalt made muddy by tractors is the head house where the serious grafting takes place. Our three female employees, the propagation crew, and Verl, El Patron, sit at a table, in crudely padded but comfortable chairs, and graft the conifers. Spanish music also plays on the radio but it is softer. A wood stove heats the room.

Isidra Villeges and Verl do the actual grafts with knives that make razors seem dull. Isidra's sister, Esperanza Pacheco, strips the needles from the sion wood and passes it to the grafters. A niece, Olivia Garcia, does other propagation and helps out where needed.

Isidra is a highly skilled propagator. She has an intuitive feel for what plants need, and the confidence to voice her observations. Verl trusts her good judgment. She and her husband, Louis, own Blue Grass Nursery. He also works at a nursery during the week. In the evenings and on weekends they tend their own business. Verl is particularly sympathetic to their efforts because he established his nursery the same way.

Esperanza and Olivia understand English but speak it reluctantly. Isidra is fluent. Verl had six weeks of Spanish in seventh grade, fifty years ago, but he has a good ear. Spanish, English, and Spanglish fly about the room. Each year during grafting season, Verl's Spanish improves. I hope that the women's English also improves.

One of my dreams was to go to one of the language schools in Mexico, for a complete immersion experience in Spanish. Last year my dream was realized. Verl and the women tease me, saying that it was foolish to travel so far when I could join the crew in the head house and immerse myself in Spanish, free. I politely decline their invitations. This nursery has a way of swallowing up people, and I want to do my own thing, not my husband's.

Verl is a highly skilled grafter. Each year he teaches grafting classes at local colleges. Occasionally visiting nurserymen drop by for a lesson. If one of them has some very rare or precious sion wood — something they found in the wilds of China, for instance — they bring it to him to graft for them. His hands are the hands pictured in the definitive manual on propagation, *Practical Woody Plant Propagation for Nursery Growers,* by Bruce Mc Donald, who is the

Director of the botanical garden at the University of British Columbia.

If you would look closely at the hands, in addition to the usual calluses of someone who works with his hands, you would see scars. They are reminders that grafting knives are very, very sharp. Each morning, Verl patiently sharpens them, another skill it took years to master. To test them he holds a thin piece of paper up and gently slices it. When he repeats the test with a hair, the knives are ready.

Verl puts a high value on speed. He moves and works very rapidly. Everyone else's pace is slow and compared to him, mine is like a snail's. When I first became a nurse, I was distressed because my fellows had finished their work when I was still in the middle of mine. But, after a while I discovered that my patients were more content than the people my colleagues had taken care of. Then I relaxed and accepted my pace. This is another reason, I don't accept the invitation to join the crew in the head house.

Every evening when Verl comes into the house, I ask, "What's the score?"

Usually he replies something like, "Isidra and I did 650 today."

Then I asked the next question, "Any casualties?" I call them casualties. Verl refers to them as blood sacrifices.

The count this year is low. Verl has cut himself four times and Isidra once. None of the wounds has been serious.

Saturdays and Sundays Verl grafts alone. He carts the television out to the head house and listens to football games. He doesn't dare graft and watch, or the casualty count would be higher.

Some of my friends ask, "Don't you get upset when he works all the time?"

I don't. Few people love their work as much as my husband. Happy people make good partners. And I am busily working on my next book.

OOPS! News flash from the head house! Verl just sliced off the end of his finger. The bleeding has stopped and it is bandaged. He is back grafting. Isidra is grafting very slowly and carefully.

Chapter 31
Family Business

The journals are full of articles about the joys and hazards of having a family business. Family relationships are complicated and when you add the complications of business to them, it can create havoc. When I did marital counseling, I frequently had client couples who were having troubles not only in the kitchen, living room, and bedroom but in the office. As we struggled to clarify their roles, I always was grateful that my work was separate from my marriage.

I'm sure your readers have noticed that I think my husband is great and we are very happy together. But I frequently thank heavens that we don't have to work together.

Verl moves quickly and decisively. I am more thoughtful and deliberate. For me, this is a time saving way to operate because I make fewer mistakes. Verl regards this method of operation as akin to watching the grass grow.

Our differences were never more evident than a few years ago when a bushel of apricots came into our possession. Apricot jam is Verl's favorite. He wanted to make it and I offered my expertise as a jam maker. Since I was still working, the task was accomplished in the evening — every evening for five nights.

Have you ever been in a kitchen — a small one — with a cross between an energizer bunny and a bull? I didn't know if our happy marriage would survive the splatters, spills, stepped on feet, and burns. However by the fifth night, we had divided the chores and things were beginning to operate smoothly.

Gosh, what I had been telling my clients really worked. Clearly define your roles and allow people to carry out their responsibilities as they see best. If this is done, diverse characteristics add strength to the team. Come to think of it, however, we haven't made jam since.

Son Paul graduated from high school and went away to college. He worked at various things, always ending up in the management ranks. Although he had worked at the nursery when he was at home and had responsibility, he never seemed interested in the nursery business.

Time passed, Paul married Julie, and our business got bigger. Our Mexican workers were doing well in the fields and greenhouses, but all the decisions and office work were Verl's. He hated being stuck in the office or at the accountants when he wanted to be in the fields or propagation house. Tentative feelers passed between father and son, enhanced by the women in their lives. Finally Verl asked Paul if he would be interested in joining the business.

Paul moves rapidly, but he is also thoughtful. He had lived with a father who worked seven days a week and long ago had made the decision that he wanted a different kind of life. They talked and talked. Finally a three page typewritten agreement was produced. Paul has been here six years and they have never had to refer to it.

A computer was bought immediately and the payroll, inventory and orders moved from scraps of paper to an organized system. Paul manages the phone and selling, and he is the one who spends afternoons at the accountants. When the need arises, he joins the crew to fill an order, but he spends much of his time in the office. Now when people call on the phone, they ask for Paul. Verl is again a happy nurseryman, close to the plants.

One afternoon last summer, the employees were taking their break under a tree in the yard and I was visiting with them. A man drove in the drive in a late model prestige car, retrieved his briefcase from the seat and approached the office door.

"I am here to see Mr. Paul Holden," he announced.

"Paul isn't here right now," I replied, "but Verl is over there by the truck."

He looked over at my gray-haired sweetheart. Verl had a wrench in his hand, and a smear of grease on his face. He was inspecting something under the open hood.

The visitor looked, his nose wrinkled in distaste, and he said, "I'll come back when Mr. Holden is here."

He drove away quickly which is fortunate. We all were roaring with laughter.

Every day when we count our blessings, we put Paul and his being here high on the list.

Chapter 32
A Few Messy Propagation Tips From IPPS!

The annual conference of the International Plant Propagators' Society, Western Region was held in Vancouver, British Columbia, last year. Verl is a member and former president and always attends. I accompany him happily because these conferences are always exciting occasions.

The motto of IPPS is "Quaerere et Impertire", seek and share, and the members do it with gusto. All day long, professors, scientists, and nurserymen share their research findings and propagation secrets. I do attend the sessions, but my main pleasure comes from meeting the people. They are a wonderful mixture of creativity, intelligence and earthiness. These happen to be the very traits that I find so attractive in Verl.

The conferences are always international affairs. Until this year, most of the people were from English speaking countries—USA, Canada, United Kingdom, Australia and New Zealand, with a few Europeans. This year, 23 people from Argentina attended, as well as people from Guatemala, Chile, and Peru. In fact an additional position was created on the Board to represent the Latin American members. Although most of the Latin Americans spoke some English, translators assisted them when necessary.

When we boarded buses to tour British Columbia's nurseries, Verl and I got on the one marked Espanol. There were other English speakers on the bus, so after an initial explanation of what we were seeing in Spanish, an English translation was given. For me, the perennial Spanish student, it was a wonderful exercise to test my comprehension. I actually understood what was being said. The tour was almost like a trip to South America.

The real members, talked plants for three days, at dinner, happy hours, and in the halls. We spouses of both sexes who were not nurserymen listened, or found each other and had equally interesting conversations.

One evening after a barbecued dinner, the traditional Liar's Forum was held. This is an open program where questions are asked and answers volunteered by anyone in the group. The answers could be based on research, hunches, or individual experiences.

The main question was, "Does anyone know how to propagate ......" It appears that there are many plants that defy the nurseryman's urge to create more of their species. One young woman, a nursery owner, asked the question about a particular plant. Forgive me, I didn't take notes and neither Verl or I remember which. The audience had questions for her. "Have you tried cuttings?", "Which rooting hormone?" When that track was exhausted they explored various seed treatments. "Did you try burning the seeds?" (Some seeds grow only after being burned.) "Did your scarify them or soak them in acid?" (This treatment simulates the natural way they are spread by passing through birds' intestines.)

She had tried all the methods suggested and nothing happened. Then an Englishman got up and said, "I have the method. I visited the garden of an old woman, near my place and there were hundreds of these plants in her garden. I was amazed and asked her how she had done it."

"It was rather messy," she had replied. It seemed that the woman had collected the precious seeds in a pan and returned to the house. While she was removing her gardening shoes, she placed the pan on the floor. Her dog rushed over and gobbled them down. She regretted losing the chance to grow more of the plant. But, not to worry, she monitored the dog for several days, collected his feces, extracted the seeds, and planted them. They all grew!

A woman, a California horticulture professor, took the mike and described a similar experience. One of her students had been hiking in the mountains, and when he returned to campus, he presented her with a package of bear scat that he had collected. She dumped it in a tray and put it in the green house. Several weeks later, it was filled with seedlings of rare native plants.

No one asked the question we all were thinking. "How does one transform this propagation knowledge into commercially feasible methods of propagating plants in large quantities?" Maybe they will tackle that at next year's conference.

Chapter 33
Practical Jokes

I have been reading *The Scotch-Irish, a Social History*, by James G. Leyburn. The Scotch-Irish were the group of lowland Scots who were used by the British to colonize Northern Ireland in the 1600's. They stayed there three or four generations and then emigrated to America, settling in Pennsylvania and Virginia. Eventually they crossed the Appalachian Mountains to settle in Western Pennsylvania, West Virginia, the Carolinas, Tennessee, and Kentucky. They formed a large part of the Continental Army during the Revolutionary War and became an important influence in American life. My grandfather was Scotch-Irish.

Now we all would like to think that our ancestors were cultured, heroic people. (Why do all my friends happen to be descended from Lord Somebody?) But the reality is, our nation was populated by the very poor, seeking better lives. The author describes the lives of the lowland Scott farmers in detail, and reading it is a humbling experience. Along with their fierce independence, propensity for settling their quarrels without asking for help from the authorities, the love of practical jokes is mentioned frequently.

My family stories are full of accounts of practical jokes, retold with relish and embellished. I know more about Grandpa Tom putting his neighbor's wagon on the roof of the barn than I do about his education or medical history. My brother spent a lot of time with Grandpa, and his jokes, often involving machinery and electricity, are quite sophisticated. The tale tellers and jokers were primarily men. Women's jokes were milder — things like baking a cherry pie with the seeds in it, or sewing up the sleeve of a coat.

Listening to these stories as a child convinced me that these pranks were not funny — they were mean. When I was seventeen, I joined the United States Cadet Nurse Corps and was sent to nursing school. Before we were even unpacked, the short-sheeting and other pranks began. I announced to the fifteen roommates who shared the apartment that I hated practical jokes, that I got really mad when someone played one on me, and that I would never take part in doing that to another person.

I must have impressed them. They let me alone. I watched my roommates struggle to bring their mattresses off the fire escapes, find their clothes, untie the dozen knots that held their duty shoes together, and remove disgusting souvenirs of our anatomy class from their beds. My stand didn't hurt my popularity one bit, and it wouldn't have mattered if it did.

When I met Verl, one of the things I liked about him was that he seemed so familiar, as though he were a man from my family. His family background is also partially Scotch-Irish. Then I began to hear the practical joke tales. So I announced my position to him. He didn't believe me.

My first birthday after the wedding was approaching. I let it be known that I wanted a gold bracelet. A nicely wrapped package appeared on the mantel the day before my big day. My spouse said it was shiny, metal and something I wanted. I begged to open it. Finally he relented. It was a shiny chrome sink stopper, a replacement for the one lost by a plumber.

Was I mad! I stayed mad all the next day. The exercise bike he gave me was hardly looked at. Finally I consented to go out to dinner. Verl pulled a nice gold bracelet out of his pocket and presented it to me. He said he had it all the time. I don't believe him. He got the message, "Don't mess with Flossy; she gets very angry."

When we were first married, he had another ploy. He would make a statement like, "Kristi doesn't need an education. She'll get married and some nice man will support her."

My response would be swift and hot. Then I learned that the spot above me on the ceiling had been made by Alice, his first wife, when he made the same remark to her. I soon learned to laugh and refuse the bait he offered. Poor fellow, he can't get a rise out of me anymore.

He is still amused when I get mad at someone else. Last November at a political meeting in the midst of a quiet discussion, a man made an insulting personal remark as he discounted my position. My manners deserted me and I amazed — and embarrassed — myself by swearing at him. The hostess was very concerned that Verl would be upset. She looked over and was surprised to see him bursting with laughter.

I don't mind a bit. Verl's amusement takes the sting out of my anger, and after a little while I sometimes join him in laughter. I guess we have evolved a long way from the days when our ancestors engaged in feuds, lived in crowded huts with their animals, and played practical jokes on each other.

Chapter 34
Landlords and Septic Tanks

As I've journeyed through life, sometimes struggling other times flying, I've learned a thing or two. (Wouldn't it be a shame if I didn't?) One lesson is that when one achieves a long sought for goal, there are often unforeseen consequences.

My husband, Verl, wanted to increase his success in the nursery business, and he has done that steadily. As the business grew, we acquired more land, buying up small farms as they became available. This meant a lot more work, but it was all very gratifying. He'd had to drill more irrigation wells and lay irrigation lines. Occasionally we had to lay drain tile. But finally the trees were planted and what had been a rundown farm was a profitable nursery.

The farms had houses on them, old ones. Initial repairs were made, new roofs were installed, and paint was applied. Our employees were our first choice for renters. This was a plus. We had someone who would watch out for problems on the place. Then too, when your boss is your landlord, you pay the rent on time.

Verl is like most farmers, a jack of all trades. Few can farm in the Willamette Valley without irrigation and that means becoming a plumber. Most farmers are also electricians, carpenters and mechanics. Add to this the depression era mentality of most of us past sixty and you have a group of do-it-yourselfers.

So in the process of becoming a more successful nurseryman, Verl has become our tenants' handyman. He moves from the role of president of the corporation, to the guy who crawls under the house, in the mud, to see why the heat vents aren't working properly. When a hot water tank blows, he is the repairman. I get assigned two tasks. I manage the appliance replacement, and explain in my halting Spanish their proper care.

The most unpleasant chore associated with all of this is dealing with septic tank problems. Now Verl is an old septic tank expert. When he was a boy in Idaho, his father earned extra money for things like the kids' music lessons, by digging septic tanks by hand. When the family moved to Salem, his father was so busy at his new job that the inside toilet project was put on hold. Verl, a freshman in high school, was embarrassed by the outhouse. He dug a hole, by hand, and installed a septic tank. I wasn't around when son Paul was a toddler, but he contributed to the family tale, "What Happens When the Kid Puts an Apple Down the Toilet."

Some of my earliest memories involve Pennsylvania out-houses. I remember standing by the kitchen door, gauging whether I could safely postpone the long walk through the snow to that little drafty house. This was followed by the pure pleasure of standing next to the coal stove to warm up that portion of my small anatomy that was almost frost-bitten from the wind that blew up the hole.

It was a great relief to move to a house that had an inside bathroom. But even then the bathroom was treated with reverent care. We had oil and natural gas wells on the property — small ones unfortunately. All around us were limestone quarries with lots of blasting. Perhaps the blasting cracked the underlying rock and let oil into the well. In any case the water had a rainbow sheen and tasted a little like crude oil. We supplemented the well with a cistern, but water and flushing were valuable commodities. We still had the little brick outhouse out back, concealed by honeysuckle vines.

After I married Verl and moved down to the farm, there were several incidents that caused me to value his expertise. Like the time when I flushed and to my horror watched the flushed-down contents bubble out of the bathtub drain. I shouted, "Verl!", and turned the problem over to my expert.

Because of our houses and the extra bathrooms for our employees, my nice husband is in charge of keeping seven septic tanks operating properly. When anything goes wrong, the users of the systems also shout "Verl!" and he rushes to rectify the problem.

Come to think of it, maybe we should reorder our priorities and honor the people who enabled us to use outhouses as tool sheds. Being a handyman for our tenants, and me, may be one of the more important roles that my successful nurseryman performs.

Chapter 35
Are There Rural Myths?

I n one of my free floating mindless moments it occurred to me that I had never heard or read any *urban myths* that concerned farmers. Urban myths are fictious stories that circulate the country that are believed by the tellers to be true, something told to them by a friend who said it happened to a brother-in-law or cousin. Often they find their way into the papers and are reported as news. Upon investigation they are found to be fantasy, much to the embarrassment of tellers and reporters.

Five or so years ago, my daughter's brother-in-law's wife told me a story she heard from someone at work. It involved the woman who came home to find her house robbed and her Doberman choking. She rushed the dog to the vet who extracted a severed human finger from its throat. When she returned home she found the robber hiding in her closet, almost dead from loss of blood and missing a finger. I didn't believe this tale but I politely held my tongue. Later I learned that it was a myth that was sweeping the country.

I did believe the one about the cement truck driver who drove by his house and noticed a convertible parked in his driveway. He parked the truck, peeked in the window and saw that his wife was being unfaithful. He drove up to the convertible, activated the revolving bed of his truck and filled the convertible with concrete. Sweet retribution! It is a wonderful story but not true.

When I was in nursing school, I heard the medical communities' favorite myths. They were usually told in the operation room during long operations by surgeons who wanted to keep the sponge nurse who stood behind him, not able to see anything, awake. There was the story of the nurse who put the x-ray on the screen backward and as the result, the surgeon extracted the patient's only good kidney. They served to make the listeners very careful. I guess the people in the Florida hospital who enacted that myth in real life hadn't heard the stories.

There were others, about finding reptiles in alimentary tracts or intestinal parasites so large that they filled basin after basin. These stories always produced a shiver of horror in the listeners, usually naive young students. I never believed them but I did shiver when I heard them.

When I was a graduate student I took a folklore course. I had to do a research project and a patient unwittingly handed me a idea. She was a psychiatric patient and was discovered to have secreted a tableware knife under her mattress. The young resident thought she was suicidal or homicidal until the orderly told us that a knife used in that manner was a common folk cure in the rural south where the patient had been reared. It turned out the lady just had a pain in her back.

This stimulated my interest in folk cures. I collected hundreds and discovered that most involved the kind of thinking we call magical or psychotic. I concluded that health care workers need to know the folklore of their patients.

Lumber men repeat stories about Paul Bunyan, but both the teller and the listener know they are tall tales, designed to entertain and perhaps instruct. Tall tales told by cowboys are the same.

I did hear one rural story that may be a myth. I heard it at an OSHA workshop, told by a supposedly well informed speaker. It was about the missing farmer who had been running the bailer. The bailer was found running but where was he? You guessed it. His remains were found, neatly bailed. The audience gasped and shuddered and determined to spread the word about safety. I did too, but I'm skeptical. Is it true? I don't know, do you?

Chapter 36
The Days of Wine and Memories

In January, when I drive by local wineries and gaze at the barren vines, I always wonder if the wine is ready. Wine making was an important family function when I was a child.

We lived in a dirty little Pennsylvania steel town during my elementary school years. We had moved there during the height of the Depression when Daddy became manager of the local A and P store. The job had been found by my uncle, a supervisor of the company, and was lost when someone higher than Uncle Jack had an unemployed relative.

Dad then adopted the fiction that he was selling insurance. He did have a connection with a company and he did make calls. But no insurance was sold. People were dealing with more urgent needs, like how to pay the rent. In reality he was a house husband.

Mother was more resourceful. She occasionally substituted for a teacher who was ill. At that time, married teachers could not hold regular jobs. She bartered English lessons for food with the women from the town's large immigrant community. She was a relief investigator and finally headed the WPA sewing room. But before all this happened, my parents sold belongings to survive. I remember that the dining room table went to pay the electric bill so that power could be restored.

Somehow money was found for sugar and Daddy made wine. There were concord grapes in the back yard and blackberries in the woods. Neighborhood fruit trees contributed and even the pretty yellow dandelion blossoms went into a crock to ferment.

One of my fond childhood memories is going down the stairs to the basement, lifting the cheese-cloth, brushing away the fruit flies and dipping a wooden spoon into the working wine. I took only one taste, but the bubbly sweet liquid was wonderful.

This was during prohibition. Daddy never sold the wine. He was not so afraid of the Federal agents as he was of the bootleggers who lived in the town. They took good care of competition. Bootleggers were easy to recognize. They were the people who had new cars and nice houses.

We had lots of company. The town's factory had brought engineers from Europe. When the plant closed these cosmopolitan men and their families were unemployed and stuck in this small town. Daddy and the men would gather around the kitchen table in the evening, sample his latest wine, and discuss philosophy, literature and politics. The women would sit with Mother in the living room and discuss human relations (translation: gossip), books, and children. It was a very stimulating environment for a precocious first grader.

In addition to the evening friends, Daddy would invite the tramps, men who rode the railroad boxcars looking for work, to have breakfast and lunch with us. The stories of their travels and struggles were always dramatic.

There was one instance when we received monetary gain from daddy's wine. One day, Mother came home about four and heard a noise in the cellar. She opened the door and looked down. There at the bottom of the steps was the water-meter man. He had arrived to read the meter that morning and found the wine cellar. This poor fellow didn't know how to sip wine like a gentleman. He must have done away with bottles of it. He was so uncoordinated that he couldn't climb the steps.

Mother closed the door and put a chair back under it to make sure he didn't stagger out into the kitchen. Then she sent my brother to search for Daddy. Dad rushed home and helped the incapacitated city worker up the steps and then took him home.

We lived in the town for seven more years, and never received a water bill.

Come to think of it, my sister-in-law (actually, Verl's first wife's sister) gave me a bottle of delicious home made wine for Christmas. It came from a barrel she inherited from her parents, labeled "Very good, 1936". Maybe I'll go and have a taste.

Chapter 37
You Know You Are Old When.......

Y ou have heard the jokes that begin, "You know you are old when...." A few years ago I discovered a new ending for the sentence. You know you are old when everyone starts treating you like a queen.

My mother-in-law, Ruby, will be 88 on her next birthday. She is a pretty little woman—just five feet tall with soft white hair and sparkling dark eyes. She and her younger son live together near here. Larry takes care of the yard and outside chores and my husband, Verl, takes care of her filbert orchard, plumbing and well. But when she needs car repair, carpentry, or some other specialized skill, she finds a local person to do it.

Often these workmen do the work and then decline payment. Ruby always reports this with a smile. "They think I'm a poor little old woman, " she says. Then she scoffs at their mistake and giggles with pleasure at their kindness.

Last December I reached a landmark birthday—one of those big ones that end in O. We went to Boston to celebrate Christmas and my big day with my daughter Shevawn, her husband, George, and their family. My older daughter, Susan, husband, Jim, and granddaughter, Leslie, arrived from Cincinnati. My brother's son, John, came from New York with his fiancée and daughters.

Shevawn sets high standards for herself and everyone else. She lives up to them. Unfortunately, I've never been quite able to. Since honesty is a trait she holds in high regard, she has always made it a point to tell me of my failings.

She has done this since she was a teenager. I am used to it and don't respond as I might to another person's criticism. I know that she loves me, and I also know that she would always do the right thing — those are her standards. My sense of humor also protects me when her tongue gets a little sharp.

We were there more than a week, with all the family, including eight active children. George's family lives nearby and visited often. Winter in Boston is cold and we were inside. Shevawn cooked for all of us and managed the celebrations with skill. At the same time, she and George were engaged in an important business transaction that involved large sums of money. They were on the phone and fax regularly, making crucial business decisions.

In spite of all the stress, my daughter spoke sharply to me only once. And wonder of wonders, she apologized. That is when I knew I had entered Mother Ruby's class. I knew I was old because I was being treated like a queen.

Now, I didn't feel old, and I didn't think I looked old — just happy — but I sure did enjoy the pampering I received.

Recently I had a similar experience. Monday morning when I read the paper, I saw that an organization I had been part of for many years was meeting in Portland. The National League for Nursing is the group that accredits schools of nursing. I had been a site visitor, visiting schools that had applied for accreditation, for about ten years. I had also served on the board that makes decisions about schools.

I hadn't known they were coming to Oregon, and I wanted to be there — to see old friends and sell my book. I called New York and learned that all the staff was at the meeting. I called the Convention Center and reached the Senior Editor of the NLN Press. She had read the manuscript for my latest book. It didn't fit into their publishing line, but she liked it and gave me a good review and permission to use it. I had never met her.

She invited me to attend the convention, free, as her guest. When I arrived, she greeted me warmly and settled me in the area where the organization's books were being sold. I saw old friends, classmates, and former students. I sold books and had a wonderful time. Then the editor, a sophisticated New York woman, took me to the banquet, as her guest. The marketing director sat with us and gave me ideas about how to market my book. Awards were being given to people who had given service to the organization and nursing education. Back at the staff table, I was feeling as though I had just been crowned.

When the evening was over, I was escorted to my car, and I floated down I-5 to home. Verl wanted to hear all about my adventure. Come to think of it, he has always treated me like a queen, even when I wasn't old.

Young Readers, don't worry about getting old. There can be pleasant compensations.

Silver Tree Books Order Form

You may order other books by Florence Hardesty by sending this form and a check for the amount listed plus two dollars for shipping.

Down on the Tree Farm————————————— $12.95

I Always Faint When I See a Syringe ————— $14.95

The Trees and Me ———————————————— $ 9.95

Send to: Silver Tree Books
P.O. Box 707
Silverton, OR 97381

Check here if you want the book signed by the author._____

If you wish to communicate with Florence Hardesty, call (503) 873-3707, FAX (503) 873-8726 or E-Mail fhardesty@msn.com.